Olivia Hirst and David Byrne

THE
INCIDENT
ROOM

NICK HERN BOOKS

London

www.nickhernbooks.co.uk

A Nick Hern Book

The Incident Room first published in Great Britain in 2020 as a paperback original by Nick Hern Books Limited, The Glasshouse, 49a Goldhawk Road, London W12 8QP

The Incident Room copyright © 2020 Olivia Hirst and David Byrne

Designed and typeset by Nick Hern Books, London
Printed in Great Britain by Mimeo Ltd, Huntingdon, Cambridgeshire PE29 6XX

A CIP catalogue record for this book is available from the British Library

ISBN   978 1 84842 929 1

Woodland
CARBON
www.woodlandcarbon.co.uk
NICK HERN BOOKS
Printed on Carbon Captured paper

Introduction

Neither of us can remember exactly how it came up in conversation, but in June 2018 we found ourselves in the loudest, most lively Greek restaurant outside of Athens, miles away from home in Midtown New York, discussing the police investigation into the Yorkshire Ripper.

It had come to light that we'd both read Michael Bilton's *Wicked Beyond Belief*, which goes into definitive detail about the crimes, investigation and, eventual, arrest of the Yorkshire Ripper.

Anyone who knows the case will know there's nothing remarkable or interesting about the murderer himself, and, like most serial killers, his story has already been exhaustively documented elsewhere. What hooked us was the audacious and far-reaching police investigation that led the charge to catch the killer. It's a story that had never been told in the deep, forensic detail that it deserved – it's arguably the last old-fashioned police case, the investigation that forced a complete rethink of hundreds of years of local policing and led to the birth of modern policing, the techniques of which soon travelled across the whole world.

So opposite each other we sat, shouting over the noise, discussing tracking five-pound notes through the currency system, hoax letters and tapes and the Byford Report. Ruining the ambience of this late-night eatery with bellowing thoughts about the biggest manhunt in British police history.

In truth the entire writing process has panned out in much the same way. Over the course of a year we've decimated the footfall of various cafés, restaurants and one very specific deli by regularly populating them; two scruffy persons buying two Diet Cokes and stretching them over hours at a time while they (we) talk loudly about policing.

There's only so much you can get out of books. When we left our favourite eateries – much to their delight – and travelled the country to meet the real people who were there, our view on the case, and the individuals involved changed dramatically.

There were two landmark meetings.

The first was visiting Michael Bilton, who wrote one of the books that had brought us together initially. On the day we were due to arrive at his door, eagerly typing his address into Google Maps, we were slightly worried that the result listed was a care home. We hadn't anticipated this and were nervous: were we about to disturb a very unwell man in his care home? On our cautious arrival it became very apparent very quickly that Michael's house was in fact not a care home, that Michael was fit and well and bursting with stories, insights and vital behind-the-headlines information into the case. Why Google listed his house as a care home remains a mystery, and he even gave us both a lift to the train station after our visit.

Through Michael we were introduced to Megan Winterburn and visited her in Dewsbury. Meg was already a substantial character in our research, having led on so many pivotal moments during the investigation, but on meeting her it was clear that Meg, or that the version of Meg in our play, would be the main anchor of our story.

Much of what the character Meg does in the play happened to the real Megan Winterburn. She did accompany Maureen Long to nightclubs on an undercover operation (only to be recognised), she was in charge of running the Incident Room at the Leeds Millgarth Police Station. She was one of the first people to hear the hoax tape when she was specifically trusted to transcribe it. It is also true that she became one of the first female officers to be promoted to the rank of Inspector in the West Yorkshire Police, paving the way for those behind her.

In fact, the majority of what is portrayed in the play is based in truth. Andy Laptew's report, the not quite above-board detainment of Terence Hawkshaw, the fact that Dick Holland didn't own a fridge. There's very little that's been added, although – for the sake of audiences – there are many things we've omitted and cut so that people can still make their last trains.

As we've researched, we've met journalists who covered the case, police officers who worked in the Incident Room, people who knew the victims and who lived through the events in the play. What has struck us is how, in different ways, the events in this play have gone on to define them all.

And the victims of these crimes are often more defined by their death than their life.

Even though our focus is squarely on the police investigation, we have had to face ourselves and acknowledge that by dramatising these events – however much we've worked to base the drama, turning points and action away from violence and sensationalism – we are, to some extent, adding to this narrative. We wanted to examine and address this question with ourselves and the audience the play will naturally attract. And even though Maureen's words, wanting to be forgotten, are borrowed from the victim of another attack, her speech to the audience is not just to jolt them – but us too.

These events were a defining moment in British cultural history. And, as we re-litigate our past and tell old stories from new perspectives, we hear the voices of those who, until now, have been silent. A new history emerges. As this play is performed, night after night, audiences will imagine women, previously defined by the usual chequerboard of police mugshots, not as victims but as real people again, living private lives, tragically cut short. Gone, but not forgotten, and no longer solely defined by violence.

In so many 'true crime' stories, the retelling spins a narrative of incompetent detectives, glamorised criminals and public order eventually being restored.

That's not the story we found. Or the one we're telling here.

The repercussions of this case defined a generation, the results of those five years still echo today, particularly in the lives of women, like an heirloom and inheritance, passed from generation to generation. Our responsibility has been to tell history accurately, to go into the detail that's often skated over and to, as far as we can, tell it how it was – not how we'd like it to be, or expect it to be. Every generation will revisit these events, and will excavate them anew. This time it was our turn, and this is what we found.

Olivia Hirst and David Byrne,
London, February 2020

The Incident Room was first performed at the Pleasance Courtyard during the 2019 Edinburgh Festival Fringe, with the following cast:

SYLVIA SWANSON/MAUREEN LONG	Katy Brittain
GEORGE OLDFIELD	Colin R Campbell
JIM HOBSON/JACK RIDGEWAY	Peter Clements
DICK HOLLAND	Ben Eagle
MEGAN WINTERBURN	Charlotte Melia
ANDREW LAPTEW	Jamie Samuel
TISH MORGAN	Tanya Vital
	& Olivia Hirst

Directors	Beth Flintoff
	& David Byrne
Devised with	The Company
Set Designer	Patrick Connellan
Digital Designer	Zakk Hein
Lighting Designer	Greg Cebula
Composer & Sound Designer	Yaiza Varona
Movement Associate	Kane Husbands
Costume Designer	Ronnie Dorsey
Production Manager	Sean Ford
Company Stage Manager	Rachel Pryce
Costume Supervisor	Orla Convery

The play was revived at New Diorama Theatre, London, on 13 February 2020 (previews from 11 February), with the following cast:

SYLVIA SWANSON/MAUREEN LONG	Katy Brittain
GEORGE OLDFIELD	Colin R Campbell
JIM HOBSON/JACK RIDGEWAY	Peter Clements
DICK HOLLAND	Ben Eagle
MEGAN WINTERBURN	Charlotte Melia
ANDREW LAPTEW	Jamie Samuel
TISH MORGAN	Natasha Magigi

FOR NEW DIORAMA THEATRE

Producer	Caroline Simonsen
Executive Producer	Sophie Wallis
Marketing	Jack Heaton
Production Imagery	Guy J Sanders
	@ Keeper Studio
Press	Gregor Cubie
	@ Borkowski PR

Thank-Yous

Julia Tyrrell, Val Day, Tom Mair, Nic Martin, Christine Langan,
Sally Cowling, Oli Forsyth, Mathilda Gregory, Andrew Baker
and Carmina Bernhardt for support with the script, story and
development. Rose Alexander and the team at Regent's Place,
and Jessica Brewster and the whole team at the marvellous
Theatre Deli for providing development and rehearsal space.
For their police insight and personal stories, Megan Winterburn,
Andrew Laptew, Michael Bilton, Steve Burrell, David Barnes &
Stuart Gibbon. And, for their general awesomeness, Rianna
Dearden, Nic Connaughton, Ellie Simpson, Anthony Alderson,
Sean Ford, James Haddrell, Rhoda and Dave Quarmby,
Monkfish, Jordan Wilkes, Francesca Marago, Murphy Flintoff,
Sophie Wallis, Helen Matravers, Will Young, Rebecca King,
and Adam Toussaint.

About New Diorama Theatre

New Diorama Theatre is an eighty-seat theatre based just off
Regent's Park in the heart of central London. Unique for its
development and support of emerging and established theatre
companies, NDT were awarded the 2019 Innovation Award and
Fringe Theatre of the Year 2017/18 at The Stage Awards, and
the Peter Brook Empty Space Award 2016/17.

Supported By

The Incident Room has been generously supported by Arts
Council England, and was produced by New Diorama Theatre,
in co-production with Greenwich Theatre and Pleasance Theatres.

For Trish and Richard
I'm lucky.

Olivia Hirst

For Val Day who wanted it first,
Mason who listened to me go on about it,
and Matravers who I missed while making it.

David Byrne

14

Characters

MEGAN WINTERBURN, 'MEG', *police sergeant, late twenties to thirties*
TISH MORGAN, Yorkshire Post *reporter, late twenties*
SYLVIA SWANSON, *civilian police employee, mid-forties*
ANDREW LAPTEW, 'ANDY', *uniformed police officer, mid-twenties*
DICK HOLLAND, *deputy senior investigating officer, late thirties to forties*
GEORGE OLDFIELD, *senior investigating officer, late fifties*
JIM HOBSON, *Head of the Tyre Enquiry, early forties*
JACK RIDGWAY, *Head of Manchester CID, mid-thirties*
TERENCE HAWKSHAW, *taxi driver and suspect, early thirties*
MAUREEN LONG, *Bradford resident, forties*

Plus pre-recorded voices from television

Setting

Millgarth Incident Room, Leeds, 1977–1981.

When the action moves to other locations, we always keep one foot in the Incident Room.

This text went to press before the end of rehearsals and so may differ slightly from the play as performed.

Prologue

Millgarth Incident Room, 1981.

MEGAN WINTERBURN *packs photographs of the victims of the Yorkshire Ripper murders into a box file. The room is empty and still. She picks up each photograph, considers it, before packing it away.*

From deep inside the room, unseen, DICK HOLLAND *speaks.*

DICK. Don't do it.

MEG. Mr Holland.

> DICK *emerges from filing cabinets and the detritus of the finished investigation.*

DICK. Megan Winterburn.

MEG. Don't do what, exactly? I'm just packing up.

DICK. Don't do what you always do. What we all do. The moment it's finished, you start raking over it. All over again.

MEG. Okay.

DICK. It don't matter how many times you go over it, it'll never turn out any different.

MEG. It might, though.

> MEG *puts the box file in an open cabinet drawer. The room fills with* INCIDENT ROOM STAFF *who, like ghosts, are frozen for just a moment.*

This time, it might.

> MEG *shuts the door and we work backwards through the years to 1977.*

ACT ONE

One

An explosion of first-day conversations are cut short. GEORGE OLDFIELD *enters. Silence falls.*

GEORGE. Five women dead. It's been my first decision to pull all five separate investigations under this one roof. Running one centralised Incident Room. Welcome. We won't be doing the usual. And we might not all like it. But we're going to work together. Something in here has been missed, and we're going to find it. Wilma. Who's got Wilma?

MEG *has Wilma McCann's investigation file.*

MEG. Here.

GEORGE. Wilma McCann, twenty-five-year-old, mother of four. Murdered night of 30th October just one hundred yards from her home, Scot Hall Avenue, Leeds. Working as a prostitute. Emily Jackson –

JIM. Here.

GEORGE. Found eighty days later – forty-two. Also working as a prostitute. Same method. No mistaking it. Then February of this year – all the same hallmarks – Irene Richardson?

SYLVIA. Here, Mr Oldfield.

GEORGE. Almost exactly the same spot. Leeds. Aged twenty-eight. Then he's on the move. Few months later – April – Patricia Atkinson. Bradford this time.

ANDY. Here she is.

GEORGE. What's your name, lad?

ANDY. Laptew, sir. Andrew Laptew.

GEORGE. Known pro. Found in her own flat. In her own flat. And now, the reason we're all here, Miss Jayne MacDonald.

DICK. She's here, George.

GEORGE. Found last week. Just sixteen years old. Just a schoolgirl. Attacked just walking home. Because this case involves prostitutes, the response until now has been – as you might expect – muted. But Jayne MacDonald, she was no prostitute. He made a mistake. And now an innocent woman is dead. Until now, Jim has been leading on some of these investigations. Talk tyres to us, Jim.

JIM. At every crime scene there have been tyre tracks. Using plaster moulds, we've lifted the tracks out of the mud to analyse them. Using the latest complex, scientific techniques, the lab is trying to ascertain the make of each of the tyres, the measurements between the wheels, between axels. Nothing like this has ever been done before, but it'll whittle down the make of car driven by our man. And we're getting that list down.

ANDY. How many have you got it down to?

JIM. We're still working on it. We've got a list of all the number plates from the possible makes of cars that could have left the tracks. And we're taking new cars off it every week. But as I say, it's a new way of working, never been attempted and we're currently at – well –

GEORGE. You might as well tell him, Jim.

JIM. It will sound like a lot but –

GEORGE. I believe it's fifty-four thousand. Am I right?

JIM. Actually – actually – it's closer to fifty-three thousand.

GEORGE. Well, beg my pardon.

JIM. But those tyres are as good as a fingerprint.

ANDY. Do you have fingerprints?

JIM. Excuse me?

ANDY. I said: do you have fingerprints?

JIM. No, Bradford, we don't have fingerprints. Only tyre tracks. It's all we've got.

GEORGE. Right! Dick? Get this sorted.

GEORGE *leaves*.

DICK. Right! Meg. Get this sorted.

MEG. Let's keep going. One last push to get everything unpacked, and filed together. Remember: A nominal index in here, The B Index, Vehicles into the C index, D index, here.

ANDY. Where do you want this?

MEG. Weren't you listening to what I just said?

ANDY. You West Yorkshire lot: look at the amount of stuff in here. I didn't join the force to do paperwork.

MEG. And I didn't join the force to deal with Bradford twats like you. Actually, that's a lie. That's exactly why I joined.

Two

TISH MORGAN *subtly enters the Incident Room. She scans the busy staff, and then seeing* MEG –

TISH. There you are.

SYLVIA. Excuse me! You can't just walk in here –

TISH. Patricia Morgan, I'm from the *Yorkshire Post*. My friends call me Tish. I was told you might – would – speak to me.

MEG. The press office is downstairs.

SYLVIA. Please, come with me.

TISH. It needs to be you. I've been told I could cover today, but only if I spoke to a… well, you understand?

SYLVIA. I'll show her out. Come on –

MEG (*softening, to* TISH). Can you keep up?

TISH. Of course. Thank you. Thank you.

MEG. Sylvia – put these in those cabinets? By last name.

SYLVIA. Bloody cheek.

MEG *tours* TISH *round the room.*

MEG. We're bringing this room together. We're all from different forces –

TISH. Is that an issue?

MEG. No… I'm from the West Yorkshire force. So is Mr Oldfield, who's in charge now. He wants the Incident Room run using the West Yorkshire method –

TISH. As opposed to?

MEG. The Bradford method. The Leeds method. The West Yorkshire method is big on paperwork. The Leeds method is more shoot first, write it up later. If ever.

TISH. That sounds familiar.

MEG. So you're with the *Post*, are you?

TISH. Yes.

MEG. And you're a journalist?

TISH. Yes.

MEG. My neighbour works for the news desk. Alan. You'll know him. Actually, I'm due to ring him. I took a parcel in for him this morning. You could say hello. (*Dials and waits.*) Hello, I was wondering –

TISH *puts her finger on the phone, cutting off the line.*

TISH. Wait. I work at the *Post*. I'm not a journalist. Yet. But that's why I'm here.

MEG. I can't make you a journalist.

TISH. A story can. Normally – normally I'd only get to write up obituaries, recipes, 'ten-minute tarte tatin'. I answered an advert saying 'smart boy wanted'. They didn't want a woman. I think I short-circuited them. So tell me, are the rumours true?

MEG. What rumours?

TISH. That you've got nothing. You're just treading water, looking busy, just waiting.

MEG. Waiting?

TISH. For him to kill again. Hoping next time he makes a mistake. (*Pause.*) Tell me I'm wrong.

MEG. What recipe is this going to end up in?

TISH. Tell you a secret. I only did one recipe. Got the oven timings wrong. Came out raw. Gave people food poisoning. They had to issue an apology. Well, I can't bloody cook, can I? Nobody died. Or if they did die, they didn't write in to say they had. He's got a name now, did you see? 'The Yorkshire Ripper'. Our copy desk came up with that. It's really caught on.

MEG. It's not that helpful, is it?

TISH. Of course it is. For us, and for you. The team that catches the 'Yorkshire Ripper'? It'll be fast-track promotions all round. This is going to be good for you. You must know that. Make it good for us both?

MEG. What are you going to write up?

TISH. I'm going to pitch a hundred and fifty words. 'The Woman Stalking the Ripper'. They'll want a mention of your hair, and your make-up. Although, thankfully, with you, hardly going to swallow up my word count. 'Functional' being only one word. No offence, of course. I'll show myself out. Nothing to be done in just waiting around, is there? (*Whispered.*) Thank you!

TISH *exits.*

Three

MEG. Hardly going to swallow up my word count…

SYLVIA. What did she want?

MEG. Promise not to laugh? She wanted to – oh God.

In the filing box she's rifling through, MEG *has discovered a cardigan sodden with mud. A moment of pause.*

DICK. Same pattern as before. Hammer to the head, clothing disturbed. Stab wounds.

MEG. Where?

DICK. Excuse me.

MEG. Where was she killed?

DICK. That's it, isn't it? She weren't killed, was she? She's only gone and bloody survived! Her name's Maureen Long, she's in The Royal. Unconscious but they think she's going to come round. Get the room ready – get these desks cleared – there's going to be a lot of information coming in. Meg, do you want me to get some of the lads in from –

MEG. No. I can handle it.

DICK. It's hard to see it, but this is lucky for us.

GEORGE *enters.*

GEORGE. Car's waiting.

DICK. She another prostitute?

GEORGE *passes some papers to* DICK.

GEORGE. Not according to her family. But why else is she caught up in all this?

DICK. We'll see what she says when she comes round.

GEORGE. Could be another Jayne MacDonald. Dressed up. In an area of known hangouts. It's the same.

DICK. Hatred of prostitutes.

GEORGE. Right! That's the link. Downstairs, quick.

GEORGE *exits*.

DICK. Sergeant, prepare the troops.

DICK *exits*.

MEG. Listen up. Listen up! Maureen Long is the first victim to survive an attack, we're asking anyone who was near the Mecca Ballroom to contact us. This is a major breakthrough. Let's make the most of it. West Yorkshire method. Everything gets written down. Everything goes into the system. One detail missing. One lead lost. And he could get away.

TELEVISION. The police are asking for anyone who was in the area of the Mecca Ballroom, in Bradford, on 10th July, between midnight and 3 a.m., to please contact the Ripper Incident Room on Leeds 464 111.

As the phones begin to ring, leads coming in, hours pass.

ANDY (*on phone*). Millgarth Incident Room, Andrew speaking. Can I take your name? And what did he look like? Just what you remember.

SYLVIA (*on phone*). And you were waiting for a taxi for how long? Okay. Slow down! Do you remember what cars you saw? Right –

DICK *sweeps in, he addresses* MEG.

DICK. She's finally awake, but confused. She got into a car. She remembers that. So every car that was in the area – every car anyone remembers seeing – I want on the map. We need it found, all the owners interviewed.

ANDY (*on phone*). Blue Ford. Number plate? And your wife was with you? Right. Thank you. Someone will be in touch. (*Hangs up.*) Eliminate the blue Ford!

GEORGE *enters. A respectful silence, except ringing phones. He addresses the room.*

GEORGE. Maureen Long has described a Caucasian male in his thirties, six-foot tall, thickset, fair hair, driving a white car, black vinyl roof.

SYLVIA (*with phone pressed to her chest*). I've got a white car here! Hello? How sure are you? Great. Okay. They saw a white Ford Cortina. Black roof.

GEORGE. And how drunk were they when they saw it?

SYLVIA. They weren't. He's a night watchman. Saw it driving off. Right. With no headlights on.

GEORGE. Jim, bring him in.

SYLVIA (*to* JIM). Transferring.

GEORGE. Dick, get a statement.

DICK. Yes, boss.

MEG. Did you say white? With a black vinyl roof?

SYLVIA. Yeah. Why?

MEG. Give me two moments.

MEG *rushes to find a card, deep in the filing systems.*

DICK. Great work – what's your name?

SYLVIA. Not noticed me then? Typical. (*Picking up another ringing phone.*) Millgarth Incident Room, *Sylvia* speaking. And what colour was this car? Oh, that's my favourite.

MEG *approaches* GEORGE *and* JIM, *carrying an index card.*

MEG. Sir –

GEORGE. Wait. It's a simple question, he saw a Mark II Ford Cortina. Is that one of the cars on your tyre list?

JIM. We've got the Corsair. It's practically identical –

GEORGE. Could a Mark II Ford Cortina have left the tyre marks at the other crime scenes?

JIM. No. But –

GEORGE. That's all.

JIM. We're working day and night on the tyres. He's here.

GEORGE. For now then, carry on.

JIM. What's that supposed to mean.

GEORGE. That, for now, you can carry on.

JIM. I can, can I? George, I just need more time.

GEORGE. Don't we all.

> JIM *leaves*.

Yes?

MEG. We did a sweep of taxi drivers for Patricia Atkinson. She liked taking taxis, apparently.

GEORGE. And – ?

MEG (*hands* GEORGE *an index card*). Of the six hundred we interviewed, this taxi was also seen on the night Maureen Long was attacked, near the Mecca Ballroom. Driver's name is Terence Hawkshaw.

GEORGE. Put it in the system, we'll get to it.

MEG. Sir, it's a Mark II Ford Cortina, white, with a black vinyl roof.

GEORGE. Give that here. (*He reads it, his mood instantly lifted.*) Dick! Look what I've got. At last, some luck.

> *We slip out of time.*

DICK. Have you had enough yet?

MEG. How do you mean?

DICK. Stop now. Come on. For your own sanity.

MEG. Stop now? We're just getting started.

> *We jump in time.*

Four

SYLVIA. Tell Andy what Mr Oldfield said to you.

MEG. He said 'at last some luck'.

ANDY. You think it's true then?

MEG. Think what's true?

ANDY. That they're clutching at straws.

MEG. Not you as well.

ANDY. They're keeping us busy while they wait for him to kill again –

    GEORGE and DICK *enter.*

DICK. Laptew. Sylvia. Can we have the room?

SYLVIA. Mr Holland, you can have whatever you like…

    SYLIVA *and* ANDY *exit, leaving* MEG *alone with* DICK *and* GEORGE.

GEORGE (*gesturing at* MEG). This her?

DICK. Tell Mr Oldfield that he can trust you.

MEG. Of course, you can trust me.

GEORGE. Of course? Right. Pick two or three of your team. Tell them they're not going home tonight.

MEG. Yes, Mr Oldfield.

GEORGE. Get her up to speed. I'm going downstairs to pull in some favours with the lads. I'll be back. (*To* DICK.) Are you sure? Women, they talk.

DICK. She's good at her job.

GEORGE. Even worse.

    GEORGE *exits.*

MEG. What's going on?

DICK. We're bringing in your taxi driver.

MEG. You've found something on him? I knew it.

DICK. No.

MEG. But, how can you arrest him on just –

DICK. We're not going to arrest him, are we? We're taking him over the road, to the Police Training School.

MEG. It's all closed up. His solicitor's going to –

DICK. He's not getting a solicitor.

MEG. Right.

DICK. If you don't want a part in this, say now.

Pause.

It's not illegal. It's just touching on it, as he put it. Your taxi man he can leave any time. We need someone to run the room tonight, to check what he tells us. You know the system –

MEG. Mr Oldfield doesn't seem to think I –

DICK. He doesn't know you. And he's nervous. These attacks, no link to the victim. Just random killing. How do you deal with that? He's thinking what I'm thinking, what you're thinking – if we don't catch him, now we might never, we might never get him.

GEORGE *re-enters.*

GEORGE. Lads are in. Is she?

MEG. Yes, Mr Oldfield. I'm in.

GEORGE. I don't expect you to understand. But we bring him in properly, we'll only have to release him again. Then he'll clean his car, burn his clothes. Get smart. And I'll be standing next to another Wilf MacDonald, identifying his sixteen-year-old daughter.

DICK. George. Come on. We'll call in when we've got him over there.

GEORGE *has left a pill bottle on the table.*

MEG. Mr Oldfield? Your wife was on the phone earlier. Shall I tell her you'll be late?

MEG *hands the bottle back to* GEORGE.

GEORGE. No. Don't say anything. Come on, Dick.

DICK. Has my wife called?

MEG. No, sir.

DICK. Funny that.

We jump in time.

Five

Night. The phones have stopped ringing. MEG, SYLVIA *and* ANDY *are waiting in the empty Incident Room.*

ANDY. No way! Let me see it! You're joking.

SYLVIA *digs in her handbag and eventually pulls out a knife.*

SYLVIA. Of course I do! It's just teeny-weeny. See? Barely a knife at all. It's a dinky little dagger.

ANDY. You hear this, sarge? Sylvia is carrying around a concealed weapon.

SYLVIA. It's hardly concealed right now, is it? Look.

MEG. She's got a point.

ANDY. Yeah, a fucking sharp one. Have you started carrying a knife about too?

MEG. No.

ANDY. Thank God for that.

MEG. I've always carried one.

ANDY. What?!

SYLVIA. Let's see!

MEG *gets a knife from her bag*.

ANDY. Bloody hell! That could be lethal.

MEG. Sort of the point, Andy.

SYLVIA. Now that's impressive.

SYLVIA *pretends to stab* ANDY.

MEG. You're stabbing all wrong. Look, you've got to go up and in. Up and in.

SYLVIA. That feels good.

ANDY. Do all women carry these?

SYLVIA. Oh yes, since Jayne MacDonald, there isn't a complete knife block left in any kitchen in Yorkshire.

ANDY. You're crazy. My girlfriend doesn't –

SYLVIA. She will. Trust me. You gone through her bag?

ANDY. No. She only carries this tiny little pink thing when we're going out.

SYLVIA. She's from Bradford?

ANDY. Yeah. Why?

SYLVIA. Trust me, it'll be like a fucking armoury in that bag.

MEG. Don't feel bad, my husband doesn't know.

SYLVIA. It was like that during my divorce.

MEG. I'm not getting a divorce.

SYLVIA. That's what I said. Both times. I hate being on my own. First time I have been really. At least Meg – at least – you'll never know the pain of losing your looks.

MEG. What's that supposed to mean?

ANDY. You can't say that!

SYLVIA. What?!

MEG. Did you get those taxi records up?

ANDY. They're in the basement. They're heavy.

MEG. Get on it. Go on.

ANDY leaves, heading down to the basement.

SYLVIA. Told you he'd believe it.

MEG. Back in the amnesty box. Bradford's finest. What's the time?

SYLVIA. It's almost eleven.

MEG. They'll be pulling his house apart about now.

A phone rings

Mr Oldfield?

Across in the Training School, DICK *is on the phone.*

DICK. It's Dick – we've got him here. Got his taxi receipts?

ANDY re-enters the Incident Room. Box files in his arms.

MEG. They've just come up. One moment.

Our focus shifts back to the Training School. GEORGE *and* DICK *have brought in* TERENCE HAWKSHAW, *a young taxi driver.*

GEORGE. You can leave whenever you want. You're not under arrest. Understand?

TERENCE. Got it. Got it.

TERENCE tries to leave.

GEORGE. Where do you think you're going? Sit down, man!

MEG. We've got them.

DICK. We can only ring out here. Start seeing if they correlate with the attacks. Find anything, send Andy over.

MEG. Yes, Mr Holland. Right, sort through this.

MEG hangs up the phone and starts handing out the taxi log sheets to SYLVIA *and* ANDY.

GEORGE. I've got men searching your house. I've got men going through your car. If they find a hair – even one – from one of the girls, that's all we need. So just tell us. Come on. Save us all some time.

TERENCE. Well, there will be, won't there? Bound to be. Hairs. I'm a taxi driver.

DICK. All the working girls seem to know you, don't they?

TERENCE. I'd never hurt no one.

GEORGE. We'll see.

SYLVIA *is the first to find something.*

SYLVIA. Meg! He's near the first one. Look – less than quarter of a mile away. Just before the murder.

MEG *places the receipt on the map, in the corresponding place.*

MEG. There he is.

TERENCE. I live with my mother, or I'm driving. I don't do anything else. I don't see anyone else. I drive all over. But I don't go nowhere.

ANDY *rushes to the map.*

ANDY. Murder number two! He's in the area that evening. Look. He's all over the place. All this area. He's here and here.

MEG. He's close, isn't he?

GEORGE. You're a bit of a loner? Nothing wrong with it. I'm a bit of a loner too.

TERENCE. I suppose, I'm just shy, always have been.

GEORGE. I bet. Like me. And shy men, like us, we don't like those loud working girls, do we? Showy. Laughing. Bad. It must make you angry too?

SYLVIA. Night of the third murder. Just streets away. This can't be a coincidence.

TERENCE. No. I'm not like that.

MEG. What about four and five?

SYLVIA. He's there for number four.

ANDY. And number five.

TERENCE. I'm not like that.

SYLVIA. That bastard. That cruel bastard.

MEG. Okay. They're all his normal patch. Around Leeds. But Maureen was Bradford.

ANDY. He's in Leeds at one o'clock night of Maureen's attack.

TERENCE. Stop looking at me like that.

MEG. Right. So not likely to have got over to Bradford –

ANDY. In Leeds, with a fare to Bradford. At 1 a.m. It's him.

TERENCE. I didn't do this.

They take a moment. MEG *is scribbling notes.*

MEG. Take this over to Mr Holland and Mr Oldfield. They're on the thirteenth floor over the road.

ANDY. Is there a lift?

MEG. What do you think? Quick!

ANDY. Bloody hell…

ANDY *sets off running.*

SYLVIA. They'll find something in his house, won't they?

MEG. Yeah. I think they will.

Our focus shifts back to the Training School.

GEORGE. So, you did know them?

TERENCE. Yeah. I – yeah – I might recognise some of them. From the taxi. Just because I know someone doesn't mean I've killed them. Does it? I know you now, I don't want to kill you, do I?

DICK. I bet he bloody does want to kill you.

ANDY *knocks on the door, out of breath.*

Andy?

GEORGE. Let me ask you a question you'll know the answer to: What's your shoe size?

TERENCE. I'm a ten.

GEORGE. You sure about that?

TERENCE. Yeah. I'm a ten.

GEORGE. Take off your shoe. Come on. Come on.

TERENCE. Okay! Okay!

Finished giving the information to DICK, ANDY *leaves the Training School, heading back to the Incident Room.*

DICK. The thing that's been difficult for us, is that these murders have happened over such a wide area. But you seem to have had no trouble travelling it. Wilma McCann – you were in the vicinity just hours before the murder.

TERENCE. Was I? I don't know.

DICK. Murder number two. And three. And four. And five.

GEORGE. Right.

DICK. And in the area an hour before Maureen Long got attacked.

TERENCE. That can't be true.

DICK. Come on. Just tell us. It's 3 a.m.

GEORGE. It's alright, Dick, I get my second wind around three.

ANDY *enters the Incident Room.*

SYLVIA. What's happening?

ANDY. Just saw the boys downstairs. They've finished with his car.

MEG. And?

ANDY. They've only gone and found a bloody hammer.

SYLVIA. A bloody hammer? Shit.

ANDY. No, just a hammer. Sorry. Lab's doing checks on it.

MEG. Get back up there and tell Mr Oldfield.

Back in the Training School.

DICK. We've found boot prints. And this is the same make and size as the Ripper's.

DICK *puts the boot down on the table.*

GEORGE. Size seven.

TERENCE. I wouldn't fit a size seven.

GEORGE. Well, let's find out. Put on the boot.

TERENCE *fumbles with the boot.*

DICK. Try harder.

TERENCE. It won't fit.

DICK. Pull it! Fucking pull it.

DICK *threatens* TERENCE *with the boot.* ANDY *arrives, panting.*

Laptew?

ANDY. In his car. They've found a hammer.

DICK. Lab results?

ANDY. Any minute.

DICK *picks up the phone and calls* MEG. SYLVIA *has entered the Incident Room with paperwork.*

MEG. Mr Holland?

DICK. Lab reports?

MEG *reads the reports that have been handed to her.*

MEG. Just been sent up. It's… it's not the hammer used in any of the attacks. (*Pause.*) It's just a completely different hammer, wrong size, wrong shape. And they've finished at his house.

DICK. And?

MEG. There's nothing there. And his mother, she's alibied him for one of the murders.

DICK. Yeah – but it's his mother –

MEG. Two neighbours have vouched for him too. And – right, yeah – he couldn't have done two of them. At least. Sorry, sir.

DICK. Hold on.

> DICK, *putting the phone receiver on the table, turns to* GEORGE *and* TERENCE, *who is still struggling with the boot.*

> It's not him.

GEORGE. You sure? Mr Hawkshaw, thank you. You're free to go.

TERENCE. I thought I was always free to go.

DICK. Piss off home, man.

> GEORGE *picks up the phone back to* MEG.

GEORGE. Right, pack up. Go home, get some sleep. It's almost 5 a.m. You can all come in half an hour later tomorrow. Nine thirty. But don't go expecting it every time we illegally detain someone. That was a joke.

MEG. Thank you, sir. I've got my review coming up. I just wanted to say how much I –

> GEORGE *has hung up already. The Incident Room empties as it gets light.*

GEORGE. Thank you for tonight. Laptew, isn't it?

ANDY. Yes sir. Andy Laptew.

GEORGE. When you do my job, you're always looking for men you can trust. This won't be forgotten.

> GEORGE *is alone in the Training School.*

> Right.

> MEG *is alone in the Incident Room.*

MEG. Right.

Six

Early the next morning.

SYLVIA. Have you heard about his wife? She's kicked him out last night.

MEG. Mr Holland? Why?

SYLVIA. She found a ciggy butt in his car, just covered in lipstick. Apparently, it all kicked off. And now he's out.

MEG. I'd offer him my settee, but where would I sleep? Christ. A whole marriage over because of a fag end.

SYLVIA. Terrible, isn't it? It was only a lift home. I should have thrown it out the window, shouldn't I? How thoroughly careless of me.

JIM *paces in, following* DICK, *who is clearly dog tired.*

JIM. Can I remind you that I am your fucking superior? Just because you're both thick as thieves –

What's going on? Are you yawning at me? Why is everyone dog tired this morning? Everyone late in.

DICK. We went out for some drinks last night. That's all. Isn't that right, Meg?

MEG. Um –

JIM. You're teetotal.

DICK. I had a bitter lemon, didn't I? Went right to me head. Kept getting rounds in.

JIM. Now I know you're lying. Do you – (*To* MEG.) give us a few minutes, love?

GEORGE *enters.*

GEORGE. No. She stays. There's too many strands of this investigation that I just don't have confidence in.

JIM. I knew it. This it then, is it? These tyre tracks are the only actual evidence we've got.

GEORGE. It's draining resources. The return isn't good enough.

JIM. The return is the Ripper's car! What's the use of resources if you're not going to fucking use them?

GEORGE. You'll need a year to get through that lot.

JIM. Give me more men.

GEORGE. Any mistakes, just one, and you might as well scrap it all.

JIM. I don't make mistakes.

GEORGE. And neither does he. Not a single solid lead. A boot print. That's it.

JIM. A boot print *and* tyre tracks.

DICK. His car isn't on your list.

JIM. You're believing eyewitnesses, who were probably drunk –

GEORGE. He wasn't drunk.

JIM. Over scientific evidence… The only way to guarantee this has been a waste of time is to abandon it now, half-finished.

GEORGE. How many cars are left?

JIM. Twenty thousand. But that's less than half – half – of what I started with! We've gone through thirty-three thousand. Thirty-three thousand. It's because I'm Leeds, isn't it? Come on, George. Don't make this mistake.

GEORGE. It's done, Jim. It's over. It's not the best evidence we've got. We've got Maureen Long now.

JIM. What are you going to do? Take her out, walk her round and see if she recognises him?!

GEORGE. No, I'm not. She is.

GEORGE *points to* MEG.

MEG. Me?

GEORGE. Don 't you start me-ing me.

JIM. You're throwing everything away to go fishing. He'll be in this final twenty thousand.

GEORGE. Nothing personal, Jim.

JIM. It's fucking personal.

JIM *leaves the room.*

DICK. We were hoping to break that to you more delicately.

GEORGE. Once she's up and about, we want you to take Maureen out. Friday and Saturday nights in Bradford. I know it's not normal to send Incident Room staff out on undercover work but –

MEG. I'd love to. Yes. Thank you, Mr Oldfield.

GEORGE. Right.

GEORGE *leaves the room.*

DICK. Megan Winterburn! See. He trusts you.

MEG. It's not because I'm the only woman copper around then?

DICK. Are you complaining?

MEG. If he's trusting me with this then – in a year I –

DICK. Calm down. It's a few nights out. Congratulations. You deserve it.

MEG. Thank you.

DICK. The moment Maureen Long is discharged, we'll bring her in and you can pitch it to her.

MEG. Wait, she doesn't know? You've not asked her if she'll do it?

DICK. You can talk her into it, can't you? Woman to woman. Congratulations again.

DICK *leaves the room.*

MEG. Thanks.

ACT TWO

Seven

MAUREEN LONG *enters the Incident Room. She shakes a little as she walks, it's clear she's not fully recovered.* ANDY *and* MEG *are waiting, ready to interview her. Despite being shaken,* MAUREEN *is full of life and energy.*

ANDY. Mrs Long, my name is Andrew Laptew. I'm a police officer. I'm going to take your description of the man who attacked you.

MAUREEN. You know the worst thing about being in hospital? Everyone is so fucking nice to you.

ANDY. Sorry, I didn't –

MAUREEN. You look about ten years old. (*To* MEG.) You, you look older – he on work experience?

MEG. You're quite the charmer, aren't you, Maureen?

ANDY. So, the man who attacked you, I've been asked to –

MAUREEN. I've always said I don't forget a face. There are some – trust me – I wish I could forget. Including my husband. She gets it! We're still together but we're not together. You know? She knows. He's been in every day visiting me, the bastard.

ANDY. Maureen, talk me through what you remember –

MAUREEN. I was born in 19 –

ANDY. About the man who attacked you. Specifically.

MAUREEN. Well, he was white. Fair hair. I think. It was dark. Not the hair. It was light hair. I'd had a drink. He, yeah, he was tall. Ish. Sorry. There are moments where it just sparks, and there he is. And – then – nothing.

MEG. Did you go drinking there often?

MAUREEN. The Mecca? I'm always in there. Best club in town. Well, one of. I was just out seeing some friends – I say friends – I mean my sister. She gets it. Tricky woman. He was thickset. Taller than me. It's hard to describe someone from memory. You don't think, do you? If I saw him, like if he walked in here right now, I'd know him. He was good looking. I know that.

ANDY. How do you know that?

MAUREEN. Because, Milk Teeth, I got in his car, didn't I?

MEG. Andy? Perhaps a cup of tea?

ANDY. Thank you. I'd love one. Three sugars. Oh, right – yes. I'll do that.

ANDY *leaves them.*

MAUREEN. Is he soft?

MEG. No, he's just from Bradford.

MAUREEN. I'm from Bradford!

MEG. You said that you'd know him. How would you feel about going back to the Mecca – with me – to see if any faces stand out?

MAUREEN. You serious?

MEG. I'd be with you. Undercover.

MAUREEN. You? On a night out in Bradford? You'd better get yourself right under those covers! Well, what can I say?! Someone offering to pay me to go out clubbing?

MEG. We're not going to pay you. We can cover any reasonable expenses.

MAUREEN. Like what?

MEG. Taxis.

MAUREEN. It's a start. And supper?

MEG. We could stretch to that.

MAUREEN. So, a cab, a night out and food. Drinks, of course. That goes without saying.

MEG. Well, I didn't say it.

MAUREEN. That's the joy of things that go without saying, you don't need to say 'em.

MEG. You're an excellent negotiator, Maureen.

MAUREEN. And – and – you'd be with me the whole time?

MEG. The whole time.

MAUREEN. I'm still the same as I was. Just the same. I just can't, I just can't, right now, I just can't be on my own. Can I?

MEG. Are you up to this?

MAUREEN. I was bored stiff in hospital. I've been in here too much. With it. I just want to get out of it. Back in the clubs. Christ, I've missed them. But you know what?

MEG. What?

MAUREEN. I've not missed them half as much as they've missed me!

Eight

Outside a nightclub, two POLICE OFFICERS *sit in separate cars, talking through their radios.*

POLICE OFFICER. Observation day twelve. Sergeant Winterburn and Long outside the Mecca Ballroom. Over.

ANOTHER OFFICER. Eating chips and – what's that – oh, it's more chips. They've got two bags of chips. Over.

POLICE OFFICER. And here's me buying my own tea like a mug. Over.

ANOTHER OFFICER. Two bags, still. I take my hat off to her. Over.

POLICE OFFICER. They're going in. Forty-three minutes past two. Over.

In the nightclub bathroom, MAUREEN *is clearly drunk,
followed by* MEG, *who is even more obviously sober.*

MEG. I've never seen anyone dance like that. You okay?

MAUREEN. You've got to just let go, and go for it. It's heaven.
You should try it.

MEG. One more hour. Okay? Your wig is –

MAUREEN. I'm fine! Don't fuss me. I'm fine.

MEG. Alright. Don't fall asleep in there. Let's not have to take
the hinges off the door like last week.

MAUREEN. I fell asleep for ten minutes.

MEG. I thought you'd collapsed.

MAUREEN. It's these pills I'm on.

MEG. Should you be drinking and taking –

MAUREEN. Don't! Don't tell me what to do. Sorry. I'm sorry.
I won't close my eyes. I promise.

MAUREEN *vanishes into a toilet cubicle.* TISH *enters the
bathroom.*

TISH. Megan Winterburn! Of all the ballrooms in Bradford!

MEG. On a night out are we?

TISH. There's not a reporter in Bradford who doesn't know
Maureen Long is out touring the clubs. Try this.

MEG. What is it?

TISH. It's lipstick, Florida Sunset.

MEG. This isn't a club tour.

TISH. What is this then? Does he have a connection to
nightclubs? Come on. Is it these specific clubs? I know,
I know, it's an ongoing investigation but –

MEG. It was ongoing until you interrupted it

TISH. Did Maureen meet him before? In one of the clubs?

MAUREEN (*from in cubicle*). Did someone shout for me?

MEG. You're alright, Maureen

TISH. Well?

MEG. Maureen isn't touring the clubs. She isn't a turn.

TISH. Not a turn? I saw her lifting up her wig, showing off her scars to complete strangers. It's the talk of Bradford. That she's going out every weekend, hanging out with some dowdy friend. Keep the lipstick.

MEG. This is an undercover operation.

TISH. I know! Everybody knows. You realise it's crawling with press out there, I'm just the only one who can get in the women's toilets. Did you see my article? I got it in.

MEG. Yeah, I saw it.

TISH. I've made you famous.

MEG. I don't want to be famous.

TISH. Everybody wants to be famous.

MEG. Trust me. They don't. You need to leave immediately.

TISH. Maureen? It's Tish from the *Post*.

MAUREEN. You alright, Tish?! Be out in a minute.

TISH. We still speaking in the week, yeah?

MAUREEN. Yeah. It's in my diary.

MEG. Are you joking?

TISH. What? She's lost her job. Thanks to your lot, everyone thinks she's a prostitute. She needs the money. And my mum went to school with her aunt. So I've got an in.

MEG. You think you're helping her?

TISH. I'm not the one dragging her round nightclubs. What? Last week Tiffany's, Mecca, Shangrila, Anabella's. Just seems random to me. What's the plan and don't tell me you're just wandering round with her, hoping to just bump into him? Is that it? Five murders, one attack, and that's it?

MEG. Do you have any better ideas?

TISH. I'm not in the police, am I?

MEG. Get out. This conversation never happened.

TISH. Bye, Meg. Goodbye, Maureen!

TISH exits just as the toilet door opens.

MAUREEN. She gone? She's a nice girl, isn't she? One last dance? Then a curry?

MEG. It'll be light soon.

MAUREEN. Good. I can sleep when it's light.

Back in the main club, MAUREEN *is in good spirits. She dances, then she turns, and freezes.*

MEG. Maureen? What's wrong? Maureen?

MAUREEN. Him. Him!

MEG. Who?

MAUREEN. Him. That's him! The man who attacked me. It's him! It's him. That's him.

The nightclub is ablaze with police sirens. OFFICERS *storm the nightclub. Two hours later,* MAUREEN *and* MEG *sit in silence.*

I'm sorry. I feel I've let you down.

MEG. Don't worry about me. This isn't about me. I'm fine. The man you identified in the club, he had dark hair and a beard.

MAUREEN. Did you tell him I'm sorry?

MEG. I think he had a bit of a shock. In your description you said you thought he was blond, clean shaven.

MAUREEN. I know.

MEG. Have you remembered something new?

MAUREEN. I don't know any more. I just wanted to catch him for you.

MEG. Don't worry about me. Although they're winding down this operation now.

MAUREEN. Thought as much.

MAUREEN *slips out of time*.

Meg… Can you imagine if we caught him then. If I'd actually seen him in the club? How different everything could have been?

MEG. Maureen?

MAUREEN (*back in time*). Well, if we're stopping suppose I'll be getting the bus home! Look on the bright side, at least now you can give the nuns that outfit back.

MEG *laughs with* MAUREEN.

MEG. Piss off, Maureen.

Nine

A meeting in the Incident Room. Full house.

GEORGE. You're disappointed. You're tired. You're feeling the strain. There's no point denying it. Some people – out there – some people – in the press – they're starting to think we're not up to the job. Scotland Yard – yes – Scotland Yard – they've been on the phone. But we're the best men for this job. You're my men. You're all West Yorkshire men now. Do you know what I told them? London. Scotland bloody Yard? When they phoned, offering us help, offering us back up? I said, thanks, lads, but you haven't solved your own bloody Ripper case yet!

Applause and noises of agreement.

So don't lose faith. He's running scared. Since this room came together he's not killed again. He's tried, and he's failed. We're going to be a step ahead from now on. We're going into his hunting ground. We're going to record every number plate in every red-light district we can manage. Someone shows up in two red-light areas – they're a suspect. We turn up at their front door. Eliminate the very few individuals punting for prostitutes and we'll be left with just one man. Now some good news, for one of you, a thank-you. In recognition of the hard graft, for the extra hours put in. For the loyalty, which I never take for granted, Andy has been promoted to Detective Sergeant.

GEORGE *shakes* ANDY*'s hand, who is now out of uniform and in a suit.*

Great job. Now, motivational speech over. Get back to bloody work.

MEG. Congratulations.

ANDY. You can still call me a Bradford twat. Won't be long till you're promoted too. Probably only be same rank for a few weeks.

DICK. Andy –

ANDY. Okay, yeah, cheers, Meg.

MEG *watches* ANDY *join* DICK *and* GEORGE.

MEG. You're a Bradford twat.

SYLVIA *approaches* MEG *holding a small wooden box.*

SYLVIA. Here's your index box for the red-light operation. You'll get more than a thousand cards in that. There aren't that many folk in the whole country punting for prostitutes!

Ten

A line of POLICEMEN. DICK *is giving them orders.* SYLVIA *and* MEG *are sorting through the first set of index cards from the red-light districts.*

DICK. Interview strategy. Phrase of the day is: Softly, softly, catchy monkey.

SYLVIA (*reading a card*). Okay, this car's sighted in Chapel Town, that's it.

MEG (*stamping the card*). File, no further action.

SYLVIA (*picking up another index card*). This one's been in Bradford... and over in Huddesfield. Dirty beggar.

MEG (*marks the card*). Action for interview. What's the number plate?

SYLVIA. It's... November, legs eleven, Telephone, Hostage, Watering Can...?

MEG. Mr James Mitchell – 16 Queens Lane.

DICK. Laptew, show us what you've got.

MEG *hands the index card to* ANDY.

ANDY. Will do, Mr Holland, sir.

A door bell.

Thanks for inviting us in, Mrs Mitchell. I'm from the Ripper team. And your name has come to our attention.

GEORGE. Keep it friendly.

ANDY. Sorry! It's nothing to worry about. Eh, this is a good chance to get rid of your husband!

DICK. First thing you need to do is get the wife out of the way.

ANDY. I need to speak to your husband, alone.

DICK. Subtly.

ANDY. Couldn't get a cup of tea, could I? Three sugars? Thanks!

GEORGE. The last thing we need is the West Yorkshire Police subpoenaed as witnesses into hundreds of divorce cases 'cause fellas are going with pros.

ANDY. Mr Mitchell – why has your car been seen driving round in two red-light districts?

DICK. You are not there to prosecute anyone for curb crawling. If he denies punting don't push it.

ANDY. I'm not accusing you of anything, of course, sir.

GEORGE. We're only interested in alibiing him for a murder. Get the alibi –

ANDY. And your employer could back that up?

GEORGE. And move onto the next.

ANDY. Thank you, Mr Mitchell.

ANDY *is back in the Incident Room.*

DICK. Andy?

ANDY. Yes, Mr Holland?

DICK. Great work. You all got it?

ALL THE POLICE. Got it!

ANDY *hands the completed action card to* MEG.

ANDY. Completed action. Alibied.

MEG. File: no further action. And here's fifty more.

MEG *hands* ANDY *a handful of cards.*

ANDY. Fifty?

DICK. Right let's get knocking on doors!

A day later.

ANDY. This can't be right, there's still loads of them, I've just interviewed a bloke I was at school with, then his bloody brother two doors down. Talk about embarrassing. How've you been? Still collecting model trains? Still into yer Lego? When you picked up that prostitute in your car the other night, did you kill her?

MEG. We've processed more than five hundred in the last few days alone.

ANDY. Five hundred men? In two red-light districts.

SYLVIA. Well, it's a bank holiday weekend, isn't it?

ANDY. Don't remind me. My girlfriend is going to kill me.

MEG. Add her to the suspect list.

DICK. Just close your eyes and think of the overtime

GEORGE. Everybody back out! Back to it!

A week later.

ANDY. There's too many, we've hardly made a dent.

SYLVIA. Here's a new box. And we've ordered a fourth. And a fifth.

DICK. You're going to need a bigger desk.

SYLVIA. How's everything with you, Mr Holland? Your new place? The divorce?

DICK. It's not that bad, divorce. Expensive like. But it's for the best.

SYLVIA. Tell me about it. After my first divorce, I went wild.

DICK. Lovely. Right, everyone back out.

A month later.

MEG. We're out of space here.

ANDY. Then make more room.

SYLVIA. How will they even know when they interview him? You go in – all best mates – and then take their wives' word for it. 'Alright, love. Is your husband, your life partner, your only source of income, a psychopathic killer?' 'No, I don't think he is, officer. Why do you ask?' 'No bloody reason at all. He's definitely not going with prostitutes. We're just here for kicks.' 'What a relief. Would you like a samosa?' 'I've not had one before' 'Haven't you? Try one, they're bloody lovely'. I mean how are you going to know when it's him?

SYLVIA *hasn't noticed* GEORGE *entering*.

GEORGE. How will we know?

MEG. Mr Oldfield.

SYLVIA. I was just saying that –

GEORGE. We'll know him when we see him. Get some rest, lads. Back at 8 a.m. We start again.

Eleven

The INCIDENT ROOM STAFF *slowly file out at the end of the day.*

SYLVIA. Night, Meg.

MEG. Night.

SYLVIA. You look… tired.

MEG. I am tired.

DICK. Let me walk you to your car.

SYLVIA. Oh, how could I refuse such a generous offer?

MEG. Enjoy your evening, you two. Whatever's left of it.

SYLVIA *and* DICK *leave*. MEG *dials home*.

(*On the phone.*) Hi, yeah, it's me – I'm staying late tonight. No, I remember. Alright. I'll try not to wake you up. Do you – Hello?

Her husband has hung up. She hangs up the receiver, and the phone rings again, almost immediately.

Thought you'd hung up on me.

VOICE (*from the phone*). Alright, darling?

MEG. Millgarth Incident Room, how can I help?

VOICE (*from the phone*). I'm phoning to talk about the Ripper. I don't know, I don't know why I do it. Why I'm ripping all those whores.

MEG. Calls like this mean real people, people in distress, can't get through.

VOICE (*from the phone*). You sound like you're the one in distress, darling. You're all alone, aren't you? I can see you. There you are. Getting warmer, colder, warmer. You won't see me. Until it's too late. You think you're getting close? This is just the beginning. And you'll be next. Stupid bitch.

MEG *is alone in the room.* MEG *puts the phone down and goes to leave. The phone rings again. She picks it up.*

MEG. Millgarth Incident Room.

The call is just silence. Occasionally a breath.

Hello? Hello?

There is a noise in one of the filing cabinets. She slowly walks over, opens it and, inside, finds a handbag with a broken strap.

ACT THREE

Twelve

TELEVISION. The body of a woman was found this morning near allotments off the Moss Side Estate in Greater Manchester. The West Yorkshire Police are staying cautious, as reports suggest this attack bears similarities to the hallmarks of the so-called Yorkshire Ripper.

The Incident Room is full of activity. The phones are ringing. TISH is trailing after MEG.

TISH (*trying to engage* MEG). Meg...?

ANDY (*on the phone*). Hello, Millgarth Incident Room. No, we'll be holding a press conference in due course.

SYLVIA (*on the phone*). Millgarth Incident Room. Sylvia. Look – listen – listen – we don't know anything just yet. We –

ANDY (*on the phone*). Hello, Millgarth Incident room.

DICK (*on the phone*). Milgarth Incident Room. Right. We don't know if we're taking statements here yet. Or whether it's going to be in Manchester. We just don't know. Sorry. Ring back later.

TISH. Meg!

MEG. I can't say. We don't know.

TISH. Manchester – that's not Ripper territory.

MEG. It's near a red-light district. That's where the investigation is focusing.

TISH. Maureen wasn't picked up in a red-light district.

MEG. No, but –

TISH. If it's him, this is going to be national news. It's going to explode.

MEG. Look around.

TISH. This is nothing.

MEG. I'm sure you'll sell a lot of newspapers. I've got work to do.

TISH. That's not what I mean. Although I think we will. You – there's already a lot of criticism.

MEG. I know. I can read between the lines.

TISH. Yeah, it's between the lines, for now. But it won't stay that way for long. Everyone's been holding back. I know I have. You must be getting closer though? The tyre-track inquiry? You must be getting that list down. Where are you now?

MEG. We've stopped on the tyres.

TISH. What? Why...? You're focusing on red-light districts, you – God – you're no closer to catching him now than when he started are you? Are you?

GEORGE enters the Incident Room, straight into MEG *and* TISH*'s conversation.*

GEORGE (*looking at* TISH). Who's this?

TISH. I'm with the *Yorkshire Post*.

GEORGE. Lovely. Get out of my Incident Room. No press in here today.

TISH. I'll call.

MEG. Don't.

MEG closes the door after TISH *leaves.* GEORGE *addresses the whole room.*

GEORGE. You'll all want to know what's going on. Dick?

DICK. Well, we don't have a bloody clue. It seems like it's one of his. But it's all the way over in Manchester. Could be a copycat. Could be anything right now,

GEORGE. We're off to Manchester. To take control. Before they come to us, and we end up on the back foot. Last thing we want is Manchester here and sticking their oar in.

DICK. Keep things running. Say nothing.

GEORGE. Especially not the press.

SYLVIA (*on the phone*). Mr Oldfield. It's for you.

GEORGE. I'm out!

SYLVIA. It's Manchester CID.

GEORGE. Great. Put them through. (*On the phone.*) Oldfield. Yes, looks that way, doesn't it? Right. We don't want anyone coming down. I'm coming to you. Well, tell him turn to back. No, nobody's here.

> JACK RIDGWAY *bursts into the room. He's got everyone's full attention.*

RIDGWAY. Morning, all. Jack Ridgway. Manchester CID. As we say in Manchester: 'handshakes are for priests, poofs and southerners'. (*To* DICK.) You're not, are you? A southerner? (*To* MEG.) I take my tea with two sugars, love. And make it a coffee. Has coffee made its way to Leeds yet? Or did it get lost crossing the Pennines, along with pasta, indoor toilets and modern policing?

MEG. Kettle's over there.

RIDGWAY. I like her. What's your name, love?

GEORGE. No point learning names. You won't be stopping.

RIDGWAY. George! I've got something you want. Jean Jordan, found dead in Manchester, body been undiscovered for ten days. It's your man alright. He tried to make it look different, but in the most obvious of ways. He's not very bright, is he?

GEORGE. From what we've seen, I think he's a clever man.

RIDGWAY. I bet you do, Georgie.

GEORGE. Six murders. More attacks. No mistakes.

RIDGWAY. Well, he's made some now. In that ten days she lay undiscovered, he returned to the scene of the crime. Why? Come on. I'm putting you on the spot, theories!

DICK. For some sick kick?

RIDGWAY. Maybe. But not this time.

ANDY. He wanted to know why she'd not been found?

RIDGWAY. It's possible. But no.

MEG. He accidentally left something behind?

RIDGWAY. You get better and better. He left something behind.

GEORGE. He's finally made a mistake.

RIDGWAY. Ten points. When he went back he disturbed her clothes, he tore up the place, looks like our man was in a right panic. He's slipped up, and he knows it. Didn't find what he was looking for though. I did.

From nowhere, RIDGWAY *produces a handbag.*

SYLVIA. I have that handbag.

GEORGE. Quiet.

RIDGWAY. No, no speak up. Speak up! Thrown over a wall. (*He throws it to* SYLVIA.) Nothing really in it. But what's special about this handbag? Come on…

SYLVIA (*hesitates*). The inside pocket?

DICK. Inside pocket?

SYLVIA. Yeah. It has a little hidden pocket inside, where you can put your – oh.

SYLVIA *pulls out a five-pound note from the inside pocket.*

RIDGWAY. Jackpot. Or I suppose, for this part of the world, bingo!

DICK. What is it?

SYLVIA. It's a fiver.

MEG. A punter's fiver.

RIDGWAY. A brand-new punter's fiver. This is what we'd refer to in Manchester as – new phrase coming up here, Georgie – 'a clue'.

GEORGE. Could have come from anyone. She could have had it on her for weeks. From some other client. And Manchester, you're miles from his killing ground.

RIDGWAY. No wonder this investigation is stalling, where is your sense of adventure? Bank of England say this fiver was printed at Royal Mint, in London, just four days before Jean Jordan was murdered. Four days. It was part of a packet of five hundred pounds. That five-hundred-pound packet was bundled in with a few other packets to make a two-thousand, five-hundred-pound bag. That two-thousand, five-hundred-pound bag was put in with other bags to make a twenty-five-thousand-pound parcel. Following?

GEORGE. I'm with you. Five-hundred-pound packet, two-thousand, five-hundred-pound bag, twenty-five-thousand-pound parcel.

RIDGWAY. Correct. The twenty-five-thousand-pound – parcel F87947 – was sent with three others – a hundred thousand pounds – to the Leeds Branch of the Bank of England.

DICK. Leeds have got a branch of the Bank of England? We've only just got a fucking Wimpy.

GEORGE. So, it was part of a hundred thousand? Good luck tracking that.

RIDGWAY. We did. Our twenty-five-thousand-pound parcel got sent to the Midland Bank and was split up. Two grand went to Bingley, five grand to Maningham, but the bulk of it, seventeen thousand pounds went to Shipley. All just happen to be in the centre of his killing ground, just in time for pay day, just hours before Jean Jordan was killed in Manchester. Pause for applause.

DICK. Bloody hell.

RIDGWAY. You're welcome, Posh Boy.

DICK. Excuse me?

RIDGWAY. Three things. One. This note was given to Jean Jordan by your Ripper. Well, our Ripper now. Two. Anyone got a camp bed? I'm staying put until we've cracked this, Georgie.

DICK. I'll put you in the cells if you call our boss 'Georgie' again.

RIDGWAY. And three. I need manpower. Fivers were given out
to thirty local firms, who put them in pay packets of eight
thousand employees. We need to talk to all eight thousand.
Won't that be fun?

GEORGE. You still don't know it's his fiver.

RIDGWAY. It's his fiver.

GEORGE (*turning attention to* MEG). You! Where are we with
the double-area sightings?

MEG. Um –

GEORGE. Speak up, woman.

MEG. There's more than we thought. Much more. We've got
tens of thousands of men seen in two red-light areas.

RIDGWAY. I didn't know Yorkshire men had it in them.

GEORGE *pauses, deep in thought. The room all looking
at him.*

DICK. What do you want to do, boss?

GEORGE. Narrow the field. Include Manchester red-light
districts – but now only interview men if their car has been
seen in three observations. (*Glaring at* RIDGWAY.) And
give him what he wants.

RIDGWAY. Top of the Pops! Eight thousand employees!

Thirteen

Working on huge rolls of employee names and numbers, the INCIDENT ROOM STAFF *start making phone calls, setting up interviews with the 8,000 employees on* RIDGWAY*'s list.*

TELEVISION. Head of the Yorkshire Ripper squad, George Oldfield, has today confirmed that Jean Jordan's murder is part of the series of murders that they are investigating. The allotment area has been cordoned off by police who are still searching for any clues that may have been left at the scene. The police are appealing for witnesses who were around the Moss Side area the evening of the 10th of October to contact the Ripper Incident Room confidentially on Leeds 464 111. Concerns that the Ripper has killed in Manchester has stoked fears in the local community. Calls are being made to clear the notorious red-light districts with police insisting that their vice squads are out in force to keep the streets safe.

RIDGWAY (*gesturing to* MEG). You, clever one, take this down. For immediate release across all outlets: Today the West Yorkshire Police are making an urgent appeal. It's almost Christmas. Families will be coming together, wives will be siphoning off money from their husbands' pay packets for the big day. I need you to check those five-pound notes – if any of them come close to the serial number AW 51 1215656 we need to hear from you immediately. Check your savings boxes, check the money in your Christmas cards or presents, one of you is about to spend Christmas Day with the monster. He's somebody's husband, he's somebody's son. He's somebody's brother, he's somebody's father. Take a look at yours this Christmas, and see if he's hiding the clue we're looking for, and report him to the police.

MEG *sits at her desk working, she's our focus, as we move through a year.*

ANDY (*putting his coat on to leave*). Merry Christmas.

MEG. Merry Christmas.

SYLVIA. Happy Christmas, Meg

DICK. Have a good one, Meg.

MEG. You too.

RIDGWAY. Up to anything nice for Christmas, love?

MEG. Paperwork.

SYLVIA (*exiting for Christmas*). I'm only having the one!

DICK. Yeah one bloody bottle. Are you coming? We're going to The Bell.

ANDY. Yep, bye, Meg.

Discreetly, MEG *takes off her wedding ring, and carefully puts it in a drawer, before returning to work. Time passes.* MEG *works on through.*

TELEVISION. Here in Huddersfield, on a freezing January night, eighteen-year-old prostitute Helena Rytka met a brutal end. Superintendent Dick Holland showed reporters the scene of this latest murder attributed to the Yorkshire Ripper. It is believed that the victim travelled to this area with her attacker before she was assaulted. Miss Rytka's twin sister has been assisting George Oldfield at the West Yorkshire Police's Millgarth Police Station

ANOTHER TELEVISION. Yesterday afternoon children playing on Easter Sunday out on this spare ground in Bradford made a tragic discovery. Having been reported missing on the 21st of January of this year, the body of twenty-one-year-old prostitute Yvonne Pearson was discovered beneath an abandoned settee.

Miss Pearson was the mother of two young children.

TELEVISON (RICHARD MADELEY). Now a lot of girls walking in the streets of Leeds in the night-time whether they're in groups or singularly, are carrying small pocket alarms, rather like this one. Now, the alarms that are on the market often make different tones… if you hear this noise, you'll know what it is. It's a cry for help.

TELEVISION. The body of a woman has been found in the grounds of the Manchester Royal Infirmary. Vera Millward, forty-one years old, mother of two, was found May 16th by hospital gardening staff. This is the second attack to happen in Manchester amid fears that the killer is widening his net.

A birthday cake is put in front of MEG. *A small round of song and applause.*

RIDGWAY. Back to work.

Time moves on again.

TELEVISION. The body was discovered in Savile Park, Halifax. Today a local community in shock, many unable to believe such a brutal attack could happen in the midst of a peaceful and prosperous area. Work colleagues have spoken of a kind, loving and generous young woman. Many too shocked to speak to our reporters. Flowers have been gathering throughout the day.

Fourteen

MEG. I need some air.

RIDGWAY. If we've interviewed everyone – where is he?

MEG. I won't be long.

MEG *goes to leave the Incident Room.*

DICK. I'll come with you.

MEG. I need some time to myself. I'll be back.

DICK. No.

MEG. Excuse me?

DICK. This Halifax murder changes things. Young women who work as bank clerks like Josephine Whitaker don't get murdered in Halifax. Nowhere is safe. I'm coming with you.

MEG. I'm not a bank clerk. I'm a police officer.

DICK. You're a woman. From now on we're carpooling. None of you girls are travelling to and from Millgarth once it's dark.

SYLVIA. You serious?

MEG. We've only just been integrated here. We're supposed to be moving forward, and now I can't even drive myself to work? Or walk to my own car. I'll add it to the list, shall I?

DICK. What are you talking about?

MEG. The list along with not being allowed to open my own bank account, or get a passport, I couldn't even get married without getting a man's permission from here. So, I thought the bar was pretty low, but not being able to walk on my own? It's a bit of a surprise. Wait, wait should I get written permission to be surprised? No problem. I'll put it on your desk.

DICK. Where's this coming from? Listen I'm your biggest supporter. But what a feather in his cap it'd be if he got you. Any of you. The last thing we need is for the Ripper to kill a police woman in the fucking police car park. I'd never forgive myself.

MEG. Of course. Because if I got murdered, you'd be the real victim.

DICK. Meg –

MEG. Apologies in advance. Especially if I get murdered without getting it authorised by you first.

We slip out of time.

DICK. What's happening?

MEG. Laid into you, didn't I?

DICK. You didn't. You're remembering it much stronger than it was.

MEG. I don't think I actually got that angry at the time.

DICK. I don't remember this fight.

MEG. It didn't happen, did it? I just said 'yes'. And you walked out with me. And we talked about your bedsit. And how you don't even have a fridge in it. And then I came back to work. But there's this expectation, that I would have been, should have been, angry, outraged. By you. By the injustice of it all. What does it say about me if I didn't feel any of that?

DICK. It was how it was.

MEG. Maybe I should have been more worked up. Do you
never think 'what if I'd pushed it just a bit more *then*?',
'what if I'd really made myself heard at *that moment*?' You
know what's about to happen?

DICK. Yeah. And there's nothing you can do to stop it. Then,
or now.

Time skips to GEORGE *talking with* DICK.

GEORGE. Dick. I come bearing excellent news. Halifax. Just
through. He bit her, the Whitaker Girl. He's got a gap
between his teeth. It fits.

DICK. Jesus.

RIDGWAY. What a clue! What a new breakthrough! He's got
teeth!

GEORGE. You! Every single one of your eight thousand
employees has been questioned. Many more than once. And
where is he? You're nowhere, man. It's time to get back to
Manchester.

RIDGWAY. Georgie, what can I say?

GEORGE. Goodbye? Just a suggestion.

RIDGWAY. What's got you so confident all of a sudden?

GEORGE. Wouldn't you like to know?

RIDGWAY. It's his fiver. One of you has interviewed him.
Someone in this team has sat face to face with our man. He's
in here somewhere. Don't get distracted.

GEORGE. Goodbye, Jack.

RIDGWAY. You've not seen the last of me.

RIDGWAY *leaves.* GEORGE *closes the door behind him.*

GEORGE. Well, that's the last we'll see of him. Megan – now.
Please.

MEG. Yes, Mr Oldfield.

SYLVIA. Please, eh? I hope you're not getting fired.

MEG. I'm not getting fired

SYLVIA. It's been so lovely working with you, such memories.

Fifteen

At DICK*'s desk.*

GEORGE. We've had a major breakthrough. He's sent us a message.

MEG. The Ripper?

GEORGE. Arrived yesterday. A tape, with his voice on it.

MEG. What does it say?

GEORGE. It's not pleasant. But it's him alright. He's sent letters too, full of things Joe Public wouldn't know. He's getting cocky.

MEG. What do you want me to do?

GEORGE. I need you to listen to the tape, then transcribe it.

MEG. Right.

GEORGE. Type it up. And get it straight back to me.

MEG. Who else has heard it?

GEORGE. Apart from us? You'll be the first. Get on it.

MEG. Mr Oldfield.

GEORGE. And, Megan, this changes the whole game.

MEG. Yes, Mr Oldfield.

> MEG *walks through the Incident Room with the tape. She puts the tape in the recorder and plays it.*

TAPE. I'm Jack. I see you are still having no luck catching me.

> MEG *pauses the tape. Composes herself.*

I have the greatest of respect for you, George, but Lord!
You are no nearer catching me now than four years ago
when I started. I reckon your boys are letting you down,
George, they can't be much good can they. I warned you in
March that I'd strike again. It will be definitely sometime
this year maybe Manchester I like it there, plenty of them
knocking about they never learn do they I bet you've
warned them, but they never listen –

MEG *presses stop.*

Sixteen

The whole room are standing and listening. GEORGE
addresses them, handing out copies of the letters.

GEORGE. This voice, the writer of these letters, listen to him,
it's the man who's been committing these murders.

ANDY (*reading*). 'I'm up to eight now, but you say seven. But
remember Preston 75.' Preston 75?

SYLVIA. What happened in Preston 75?

GEORGE. A murder. That's what happened in Preston. The first
Yorkshire Ripper murder.

DICK. Joan Harrison – not a known prostitute –

GEORGE. – but – but – known to take money from men, for
sex, to feed her drinking habit.

DICK. Head injuries. Clothing disturbed. Severely beaten,
and –

GEORGE. He bit her. Clear bite mark with –

MEG. – a gap in his teeth?

GEORGE. Clear as day. Just like the Whitaker girl in Halifax.
And the second giveaway – if you needed one – he left
semen. From which they could determine his blood type.

Blood type B secretor. Rare. Extremely rare. Only six per cent of the population have it. You tell them, Dick.

DICK. Whoever sent the tape, he made sure to leave no fingerprints, he's even put the tape together from several parts of different cassettes. He thinks he's smart. But he licked the seal of the envelope, didn't he? We've managed to get enough saliva off it to determine his blood type.

GEORGE. It's a match, B secretor!

A celebration ripples through the meeting. A breakthrough at last.

The man who wrote that letter, the voice on that tape, he killed Joan Harrison in 1975 in Preston. And he's been killing ever since. We find that voice and it's all over. Finally.

MEG. There's a problem. With this letter.

GEORGE. Excuse me?

MEG. Yvonne Pearson. This letter was sent just before her body was discovered. But she was there, undiscovered for a long time. Right? She was already dead when this letter was written, but not discovered until after it arrived. But then why doesn't he mention her?

GEORGE. Why? You don't think I've considered that?

MEG. I –

GEORGE. I'm talking. You're listening. Her murder was different to the others. I've never been comfortable including it in the sequence. She was killed by a blow to the head by a rock. Not a hammer. When you look at it – yeah, when you look at it – Preston 75 is much more in keeping with the rest of the sequence.

MEG. But on the tape he says eleven now. So includes Yvonne Person in his total. But not in the earlier letter. Doesn't make sense? Why would he do that?

GEORGE. Doesn't make sense? Does it make sense that he's smashing women like you to pieces? Although I'm starting to see it. You – you don't think I've thought about all of this?

I'm living this case, second to second. You don't take this
case home like I do. You think I've –

DICK. George –

GEORGE. Back off. We're all getting too familiar here. The
only thing you should be doing is shutting up and doing your
typing. Look at this room! How can anyone think in here?
Get this down.

MEG. Now?

GEORGE. Yes now. Of course, now.

We slip out of time. MEG *looks at* DICK. *Neither says
anything.*

MEG. Yes, sir.

We're back in the room. MEG *sits typing as* GEORGE
dictates.

GEORGE. If a suspect is not born between 1924 and 1959, he's
not our man. Eliminate him from the inquiry. If he's not
white. Eliminate him. Shoe size nine or above. Eliminate
him. If he doesn't have a B secretor blood type. Eliminate
him. Handwriting doesn't match these letters. Eliminate him.
If he doesn't have a Geordie accent. The accent on this tape.
Eliminate him. Type it up, circulate it, and stick to it. You lot
don't know good news when you hear it. Christ, this force
has gone to the dogs.

DICK. George –

GEORGE. You're either working for this investigation or
against it. We're calling a press conference. We're releasing
the tape to the public. Decision made.

*GEORGE exits the Incident Room as the media start to
report on the tape.*

CONTINUITY VOICE (*on the radio*). Before we continue with
tonight's schedule, an urgent bulletin from the West
Yorkshire Police.

GEORGE (*on the radio*). This is the voice of the Yorkshire
Ripper:

TAPE (*on the radio*). I'm Jack. I see you are still having no luck catching me. I have the greatest of respect for you, George, but Lord! You are no nearer catching me now than four years ago when I started.

Phones begin to ring.

GEORGE (*on the radio*). If anyone recognises this voice, contact the Millgarth Incident Room immediately on 464 111.

TISH *enters to find a room in chaos.*

TISH. Is it really him? Is that really his voice?

MEG. They think it's him.

TISH *hands* MEG *a copy of the* Yorkshire Post, *the front-page story is the tape.* MEG *begins to read.*

NEWS READER (*on television*). A development in the hunt for the Yorkshire Ripper. George Oldfield releases a tape with the killer's voice.

TAPE (*on television*). I'm Jack. I see you are still having no luck catching me. I have the greatest of respect for you, George, but Lord!

SYLVIA (*on the phone*). Okay – okay. We've set up a hotline, if you ring this number, you can hear the full tape. Got a pen ready?

MEG. It's on every page. The tape is being played in cinemas –

TISH. – in schools,

MEG. In nightclubs, on the news first thing in the morning, last thing at night. Head of the investigation George Oldfield has said –

We see GEORGE *giving a press conference.*

MEG/GEORGE. He's playing us all for fools.

GEORGE. We at the West Yorkshire Police will not stop –

TISH. Will not rest –

GEORGE. We will not sleep –

MEG/GEORGE/TISH. Until we find the man on that tape.

GEORGE. He's called me out by name. He's made it personal. And now I'm coming for him, with everything I've got.

The phones all start ringing at once. The voice is everywhere. It overwhelms the room.

Blackout. In the darkness we hear the final sentence on the tape...

TAPE. Well, it's been nice chatting to you, George. Yours, Jack the Ripper.

Interval.

ACT FOUR

Seventeen

The Incident Room is now full of paper. ANDY *is working, exhausted.* MEG *enters. It's early in the morning.*

MEG. Morning.

ANDY. You're here early.

MEG. Go home. Get some sleep.

ANDY. Nothing interesting. Drunks till about 1 a.m., then trouser fiddlers, disappointed to get a man picking up.

MEG. Well, I'm here now, aren't I?

ANDY. Meg? I've met someone.

MEG. I'm delighted for you.

ANDY. No. A man. I interviewed him, he's a triple-area sighting in the red-light districts.

MEG. Him and all the rest of Yorkshire. We've interviewed fourteen bishops.

ANDY. No, I know I've seen thousands, we all have by now, but he's really bothering me. I can't stop thinking about him.

MEG. Speak to Mr Oldfield.

ANDY. I want to make it into a report. I need someone to type it for me? Help me get it together. Help give it the best chance? I wouldn't ask, but it's important. I want to do it right.

MEG. If I get a minute, fine.

ANDY. Thank you, thank you, thank you!

MEG. Go home and get some sleep.

ANDY. Night, Meg.

MEG. Morning, Andy.

> MEG *moves a box file and finds* GEORGE *half-asleep. He's been there all night.*

GEORGE. What time is it?

MEG. Just after six, sir.

GEORGE. I must have fallen asleep. I'm awake. I'm awake now.

MEG. Are you okay?

GEORGE. I'm fine. Just need to take – where are they? (*Spotting his pills.*) Here we are.

MEG. Should you be taking those with coffee, sir?

GEORGE. It's not coffee. It's whiskey. Ah. That's better.

MEG. Do you want me to get a car to take you home?

GEORGE. No, I'm here now.

MEG. Or call your wife?

GEORGE. She's used to it. I normally sleep in my office so – right – what are we looking at today? Get me some water.

MEG. I think that's a good idea.

> MEG *fetches a glass of water.*

GEORGE. They think he's from Castletown, the voice experts. The voice on that tape comes from Castletown. Small mining village off the weir.

MEG. I know, sir. Here, Mr Oldfield.

> GEORGE *washes himself with the water.*

GEORGE. We need to interview every male between twenty and sixty-five in Castletown.

MEG. We have, sir.

GEORGE. We need the birth registers, the parish records.

MEG. They're on my desk. All checked, sir. Are you sure you don't want –

GEORGE. We need to get that tape out there. I don't want anyone in Yorkshire to have not heard that voice.

MEG. Why don't you sit down, Mr Oldfield. It's everywhere, sir. We've got teams playing it in cinemas, on the radio, on the television. Every Friday night it's played in nightclubs, it's been played in old people's homes. It's played in schools. I don't know anyone who can't recite that tape.

GEORGE. So where is he? A million spent on advertising. Where is the man with that voice?

MEG. You should get some rest.

GEORGE. That's what he wants. That's exactly what he wants. I'm Jack. I see you are still having no luck catching me. I have the greatest of respect for you, George, but Lord! You are no nearer catching me now than four years ago when I started. I reckon your boys are letting you down, George, they can't be much good can they.

A phone rings. MEG *answers.*

MEG. Millgarth Incident Room –

Mud pours out the receiver, she looks over to GEORGE. DICK *enters.*

DICK. Here you are. I've been calling you at home.

GEORGE. I came in early. Get a good start.

DICK. There's been a body found. In Bradford. A student.

GEORGE. He said October in the letter and here we are.

DICK. Car's downstairs. I'll wait for you.

GEORGE. Bradford.

DICK. We'll send through information when we've got it. Press conference, let's say in four hours? Can you set it up?

MEG. Of course.

DICK. Brief the others when they arrive.

MEG. Yes, Mr Holland.

DICK *exits.*

GEORGE. Bradford. Bloody Bradford again. I'll tell you where he lives. I know where he lives. He lives up here. And he never bloody sleeps.

GEORGE *exits*.

Eighteen

The room fills and empties again across the course of the day.

TELEVISION. Welcome to the lunch-time news. Today in Bradford the search for missing student Barbara Leach has ended in tragedy. The latest victim of the Yorkshire Ripper.

In a few hours the West Yorkshire Police will hold a press conference at the Millgarth Police Station to update press and public on this latest tragic killing. Barbara, age twenty, was about to start her third and final year at the Bradford University studying a degree in social psychology. She had been enjoying a drink with university friends in the Manville Arms. She and the group left at around 12:45 a.m. with Barbara opting to walk home.

SYLVIA. I'm going down to listen. Coming?

MEG. No, I'll stay here.

TISH *enters*.

SYLVIA. Suit yourself. You again? Don't they teach you directions at the *Post*? Press room is downstairs.

TISH. I'm here to see her. And it's the *Daily Mirror* now.

SYLVIA. Well, excuse me, your majesty.

SYLVIA *exits*.

MEG. What do you want?

TISH. This is never going to end, is it? You look like you've given up.

MEG. We haven't given up.

TISH. Is this honestly the best you can do? It's what everyone is asking. The people here to protect us – is the best they can do? It's been years. He's killing students now. Getting braver. Bolder. If it was me, I'd be laughing. Because whatever he does, you can't catch him.

MEG. The press conference is downstairs. You're missing it.

TISH. I've been to enough of them. I can't sit through another one. The same old words, same promises, and then a few months later, we're back again. If it wasn't so sad, so horrible, it'd be embarrassing. That's why you're not down there either. Even though you'll never admit it. Here. My old colleagues at the *Post* have published this. Out next week. You've taken so long to catch him, there's been time to write and have a book published.

She fishes out a copy of I'm Jack, *written by Frank Smyth and Peter Kinsley.*

It's a profile of your man. All the key dates. Everything known so far. I've come to ask for a comment. They've given me the national exclusive. Pre-sales are through the roof, apparently.

MEG (*reading from the book*). '*I'm Jack* is the macabre and terrifying true story of a police manhunt for the most elusive of all murderers – the psychopathic, compulsive killer. And he's still at large.' This isn't journalism. It's entertainment, titillation. You realise the Yorkshire Ripper, he doesn't actually exist?

TISH. Excuse me?

MEG. He's not real. He was Frankensteined together in your newsrooms. This is about a monster. We're looking for a man, a normal man.

TISH. Eleven women are dead. And you say he's not a monster!

MEG. Think. If we were looking for a monster we'd have found him by now.

TISH. Since I started looking, I see nothing but monsters. Number one in the charts right now is a song called 'Killer on the Loose'. 'Don't unzip your zipper, 'Cause you know

I'm Jack the Ripper.' All the films are all about women
getting ripped apart. Every time Leeds United play their
chanting 'There's only one Yorkshire Ripper.' That's what
men want to watch, want to listen to. That's who they really
are. Nothing's really changed. Every bit of progress you
think you've made, it's lip service. The smallest bit of
pressure pushes down – one man – and you've got to be
escorted to work, even if you're in the police. They'll be
banning us going out at all next.

MEG. No that's – look at us. Here. We are progress. A female
copper. A –

TISH. We? You're one of the very few who've been allowed in
the club. And what a fat lot of good that's doing us. We've
got a female Prime Minister – so it must be fine for us all.
Me and her. We're just the same, right? I'll put my feet up.
Job done. Wake up. Nothing's changed if you look like I do.
Or if you're not an 'innocent' women, or you're just not
'decent', whatever that means, if you aren't the right sort of
woman. We all deserve what we get. That's fine. That's fair
enough. You go along with the men. I tell you one thing
though, a society that thinks it's fine for a man to attack and
kill certain women, sure as hell can't produce a police force
capable of catching him.

The INCIDENT ROOM STAFF *begin to enter back in.*

MEG. Press conference is over. Are you done?

TISH. Women like me? We're just getting started. (*Seeing*
GEORGE *and* DICK *walk past.*) Mr Oldfield!

DICK. Not now, Meg!

TISH *sits down, it's clear she's not moving until she gets
what she came for.*

TISH. Get me a quote from George Oldfield, about the book.
It's what I've come for. Just a line. And, then, I'll go.

MEG. Wait there.

MEG *approaches* GEORGE *and* DICK. *Closer, it's clear*
GEORGE *is in physical pain.*

I'm sorry to –

GEORGE. I don't want her knowing –

MEG. What's wrong?

DICK. Relax, George. Calm and breathe. Not a good time, Meg.

MEG. Is he having a…?! Have you called an ambulance?

GEORGE. I'm not having them see me taken out of here in an ambulance. I'm not having them know he's done this to me.

DICK. A taxi is meeting us outside. Stay sitting down!

GEORGE. Dick, if they find out, they'll take me off this.

DICK. I need your help getting him out. His wife's waiting at the infirmary. I'll take him down the back stairs.

MEG. Tish Morgan is here. The journalist.

DICK. And downstairs is crawling with them. Christ. You need to make sure she doesn't see this. Come on, George.

MEG *and* DICK *lift* GEORGE *up*. DICK *takes him.*
DICK *leads* GEORGE *through the Incident Room, subtly supporting his walk.*

TISH. Mr Oldfield. I said, Mr Oldfield. Is he ignoring me? You're acting like schoolchildren. Scuttling away like that.

MEG. I'm afraid it's a no.

TISH. Of course it is. Tell your boss he's going to regret pissing me around. I'm a female journalist. One day it's going to be me writing his obituary.

TISH *exits.*

MEG. Might be sooner than you think.

ANDY. What's all that about?

MEG *hands* ANDY *the typed report.*

MEG. Here. It's good. I'm not doing any more typing for you.

ANDY. You really think it's good?

MEG. He doesn't fit the elimination criteria.

ANDY. No, he doesn't.

Nineteen

DICK *re-enters*.

DICK. What a bloody long day. It's not even four o'clock yet.

ANDY. Has Mr Oldfield gone?

DICK. He's been called away on a family emergency. Talk to me.

ANDY. When will he be back?

DICK. How long is a piece of string, Andy?

ANDY. Maybe I should wait. Sorry to bother you, sir.

DICK. I don't have time for this. I said talk to me.

ANDY. I've got something.

DICK. What? Give that here.

DICK *takes the report from* ANDY*'s hands*.

ANDY. I met someone who – well, it's just a hunch – he doesn't feel right. I interviewed him as part of the red-light inquiry. He's just –

DICK. Handwriting sample? Come on!

ANDY. Yes – there was one on file –

DICK. And does it match?

ANDY. No, but –

DICK. Bradford? He's from Bradford? Does he even have a Geordie accent?

ANDY. No. But –

DICK. How much time have you pissed away on this? Have you been listening in any of the briefings? You've never listened though, have you? Never been totally on top of the job.

ANDY. Come on, sir.

DICK. No, I've tried encouraging you, taking you under me wing. And for what? To be embarrassed by slack work like this. Who typed this up for you? Sylvia?

SYLVIA. Don't look at me.

DICK. Well, somebody typed it. It weren't him, was it?

ANDY. Meg helped me to – his name's Peter William Sutcliffe.

DICK. I don't care if he's legally changed his name to the Yorkshire Fucking Ripper. It's not him, is it? He doesn't fit anything we've done. This is why we're not getting anywhere. None of you are working together. Maybe you're incapable of it.

ANDY. I thought –

DICK. You thought – I don't give a flying fuck what you thought.

ANDY. He looks like some of photofits.

DICK. So, does half of Leeds and two thirds of Bradford. Photo fit? Photofit?! I look like some of the fucking photofits. If someone else comes to me saying photofit again they'll be back in uniform doing traffic until their retirement. What is wrong with you all? Meg – how long did this take you? To type up?

MEG. A couple of hours earlier today –

DICK. Today? With everything that's been going on? You have nothing better to do that type up this rubbish? I thought you'd know better. Obviously not. Christ. Stay late. Make up the time. And take a good look at yourselves.

As evening falls, the team leave. Afternoon turns to late evening.

Twenty

MEG *sits alone reading* I'm Jack. *Sheepishly,* DICK *enters.*

DICK. Do us a favour – flick to the end and tell me whodunit.

Long pause.

MEG. How's Mr Oldfield doing? How's his indigestion?

DICK. Stable. Things have got a bit hot in here. I wanted to
apologise.

MEG. Things are hot everywhere. I've stopped telling people
I'm police. It's funny, I've been trying for weeks to get a
moment with you. About Andy's promotion. The latest one.

DICK. The Andy Laptews of the world, it's what they do, isn't
it? Look at him. He was always going to rise up fast. You,
you're special –

MEG. Don't give me that.

DICK. You run this room well. Nobody else can, If we promote
you, who'd replace you? We'd be stupid to do it. Take it as
a compliment.

MEG. This isn't going to be fine, is it? The tape is right. We are
no closer to catching him than when we started.

DICK. It's late.

MEG. You should go home. There's no need for you to be
reading those statements yourself.

DICK. We got to get through it. Since the tape, those letters, if
I don't clear this lot, there's just too much…

MEG. There's nothing in those letters that wasn't public
knowledge. It's all in here. They've not seen the letters – but
I have. All the details we thought only the killer would know.
Was all in papers. We've interviewed everyone in
Castletown. Nothing. What do we actually know about him?

DICK. Well. (*Pause.*) He hates prostitutes –

MEG. Or just women. Prostitutes are just an easy target. What
else?

DICK. His shoe size. His – well, he's got teeth – (*Pause.*)
We don't know a thing

MEG. 'You are no closer to catching me than four years ago
when I started.'

DICK. We can't go back. The public are sure that tape is him,
the boss is sure it's him –

MEG. Are you?

DICK. George Oldfield is a good man.

We slip out of time.

MEG. Think, I could have stood up right then, taken just few
steps and picked up a piece of paper with his name on it. If
only we'd known where to look. Every time I relive it I push
myself harder and harder, to get through more of it, because
I think I might get there. To his name.

DICK. Every time?

MEG. I've been over this so many times. I've lived a whole
life. I am an old woman. And yet I'm sitting in my chair at
home, right now, and I'm going over it all again, aren't I?
I've never left this room. When my granddaughters come to
see me –

DICK. Granddaughters?

MEG. They come in. I take off their coats, and their boots and
they say 'Grandma, can you tell us about the Ripper?' I never
leave this room.

DICK. We didn't admit it then. But we were nowhere.

MEG. Not true.

They slip back into time.

That five-pound note was the only lead we had really. Did
we throw our chance away?

RIDGWAY *bursts in.*

RIDGWAY. Fuck me, you both look like zombies!

DICK. Bloody hell!

RIDGWAY. You! Were you and Posh Boy just thinking about our five-pound note? Typical Yorkshire man, always thinking about money. As they say in Manchester: 'I'm glad I'm not in charge of running this albatross of an inquiry'. Where's Oldfield?

MEG. He's not here.

RIDGWAY. Makes sense, I thought I didn't smell something.

DICK. He's in the hospital, man.

RIDGWAY. Well, while the cat's away, let's play. Dust yourselves off, put your pants back on, I've got a few new ideas for our punter's fiver. Right! Gather around!

Twenty-One

Daytime. RIDGWAY *throws a bag of dummy notes onto the table.*

RIDGWAY. This, my Yorkshire friends, is twenty-five hundred dummy notes all printed and marked up. Identical in every way, serial numbers and all, to our favourite parcel, parcel F87947.

DICK. Are you serious?

RIDGWAY. Courtesy of Her Majesty's Royal Mint.

DICK. How did you get them to do that?

RIDGWAY. Have you been out there? Have any of you? This is a national crisis. If they didn't help now, they'd be strung up. I'm going to lead a full recreation of those three days between our note being printed and Jean Jordan's murder. Using the bank ledger books, now we've got these five-pound notes in the exact order they were printed, we can recreate every single transaction, every note issued, at the bank. Until we put our five-pound note into the hand of our man.

DICK. That'll take you weeks.

RIDGWAY. Well, you've had years. Plus, isn't it just good to see me?

They begin working through the bank ledger books with the dummy five-pound notes.

ANDY. Meg, Maureen Long is here to see you.

MAUREEN *enters.* MEG *and her sit alone.* MAUREEN *is very different, only a few years later.*

MAUREEN. You look as tired as I feel.

MEG. You still getting out and about?

MAUREEN. I don't go out. I don't do much of anything now.

MEG. Have you remembered something?

MAUREEN. No. My head aches when I try, I've tried so hard.

MEG. Why did you want to see me?

MAUREEN. I'm just back from London. A coach trip. The others were pissing me right off so much I went on my own and I came to this huge graveyard they were digging up. I got talking to the men – I still can talk to anyone – and I said 'who's that?' 'Cause they'd left one grave alone in the middle of the graveyard, cordoned it off and left it. I thought it would be some big man, but it were one of the women that Jack the Ripper killed. A hundred years ago. That's why they're keeping it. And I thought, you know, I thought, 'that's me'. That's all I am now.

MEG. That's not true.

MAUREEN *pulls out the* I'm Jack *book.*

MAUREEN. When he hit me, he didn't kill me. But my life stopped there, didn't it? Oh, here it is, I'm in it. Read it. Out loud. Read it to me.

MEG (*reading*). 'Swinging her imitation leather handbag, Mrs Long sauntered past the taxi queues down towards the centre of Bradford.'

MAUREEN. He's not been caught, he's still killing, and there's already a bloody book. It's just the first. Course it is. I can't stop shaking, I can't hold down a job. I can't watch telly, the news, anything violent, I have fits, I can't sleep. And I can see them all, all laid out into the future. The books, the newspapers, the films. It'll never stop. I know it won't. I can see it. Like I can see you. You don't know who I am. I didn't want this. But you could make it go away. I need you to do something. I need you to come out and say he didn't do this to me.

MEG. I don't understand.

MAUREEN. I want you to come out and say you made a mistake. And I'm not one of the list. I want to be forgotten. You could do that.

MEG. We can't. I'm sorry, it's just –

MAUREEN. There's other folk the papers say what are desperate to be on the list, they're sure they were attacked by him, so just take me off it and put them on.

MEG. It's not possible.

MAUREEN. You're just the same really. He's stained you lot an' all. Nobody will ever look at the coppers the same way again.

MEG. We've got a new line of inquiry. I think –

MAUREEN. I think it's great. That you can still be optimistic. I can't. I hope for your sake that it comes off. It'll be your last chance. What's the point of having police at all? What's the point of any of you?

MEG. Maureen –

MAUREEN. Call me when – when! If! – if you catch the bastard. You know where I am. I'm not going anywhere.

MAUREEN *exits*.

Twenty-Two

RIDGWAY. I have to say, I'm impressed. It's taken weeks, we've played every banker, cashier and customer but I think it's been worth it. Drum roll please. Come on, stamp your feet. We've narrowed our suspects down from eight thousand men to – come on – just two hundred and forty!

A stunned silence. Then a round of applause. In amongst the applause, GEORGE *enters.*

GEORGE. What a welcome back!

DICK. George.

MEG. Mr Oldfield.

RIDGWAY. Georgie! Porgie! Pudding and pie. Got indigestion and didn't die!

GEORGE. What's he doing here?

DICK. We've re-run the five-pound-note inquiry, we've got it down to a list of two hundred and forty –

RIDGWAY. Two hundred and forty!

DICK. Whoever gave the fiver to Jean Jordan is on that list.

GEORGE. You seem sure. Any of them promising?

ANDY. Actually, Mr Oldfield, sir. Mr Ridgway –

GEORGE/RIDGWAY. Yes?

GEORGE. Yes?

ANDY. I wrote a report for you, sir. Before you left. About a Peter William Sutcliffe.

DICK. Andy – I –

ANDY *hands his report to* GEORGE, *who reads it.*

ANDY. He's on the list of two hundred and forty.

DICK. He is?

SYLVIA. I was looking up the name in the filing system. And I found Andy's report filed with his cards.

MEG *goes to the nominal index and pulls out a folder.*

DICK. Meg?

MEG *plants the folder on her desk and reads the paperwork as she pulls it out.*

MEG. Peter William Sutcliffe. Seen over thirty times in red-light districts. Peter William Sutcliffe. Interviewed in the first five-pound-note inquiry, twice. Peter William Sutcliffe. His car, a white Ford Corsair is part of the tyre-track observations. On Jim Hobson's list of twenty thousand. He's been picked up in every investigation.

ANDY *has gone to pull out the photofits from the surviving victims and witnesses.*

ANDY. And look at the photofits.

MEG. Dark hair, beard, just like the man Maureen picked out in the nightclub.

RIDGWAY. Well, look at that.

GEORGE. Accent? Handwriting?

DICK. Meg – what are you doing?

MEG. Not a match.

GEORGE. So, it can't be him.

MEG. But he was arrested in the red-light district, just as the murders were starting. We checked his record.

GEORGE. And –

MEG. Cautioned for going equipped for burglary.

GEORGE. Why equipped for burglary?

MEG. Because they found him with a hammer.

GEORGE. Christ. Get the cars. We're going for him. Dick, this is it, isn't it?

DICK. Meg –

GEORGE. We've done it. We've all done it. I always said I'd know him when I saw him. And I'm seeing him now. We've got him!

We slip out of time.

DICK. This isn't what happened.

MEG. It's what should have happened.

DICK. You're torturing yourself.

MEG. His name was on that list. On a list of two hundred and forty. And when we went to his file – it should have been teeming with all this information. And instead – there was nothing there. How could there have been nothing there?

DICK. I don't know. Meg…

MEG. Just let me. Just for a second.

Time resumes.

Well done, Mr Oldfield. Well done, Sylvia. Andy.

ANDY. Thank you, Meg.

MEG. Mr Ridgway.

RIDGWAY. I couldn't have done it without you! Actually, could I have? Maybe.

GEORGE. The system worked. The hours you've spent, the frustrations, the fear, none of it has been in vain.

We slip out of time again.

MEG. And, Mr Holland. Well done to you too.

DICK. And to you.

MEG. Okay. I'm ready.

Rewind.

Twenty-Three

RIDGWAY. Two hundred and forty!

A stunned silence. Then a round of applause. In amongst the applause, GEORGE *enters.*

GEORGE. What a welcome back!

DICK. George.

MEG. Mr Oldfield.

RIDGWAY. Georgie! Porgie! Pudding and pie. Got indigestion and didn't die!

GEORGE. What's he doing here?

DICK. We've re-run the five-pound note inquiry, we've got it down to a list of two hundred and forty –

RIDGWAY. Two hundred and forty!

DICK. Whoever gave the fiver to Jean Jordan is on that list.

GEORGE. You seem sure. Any of them promising?

There's a silence.

I thought not. We'll be in touch if we need anything.

RIDGWAY. I'll stay.

GEORGE. No need by the sounds of things. And I'm back now. I'll say this: if I was a Geordie on that list, I'd be bloody nervous. When we catch him – you'll be the first to know. Well. Top ten. And make it two hundred and forty-one on that list.

RIDGWAY. Who's the one?

GEORGE. Terence Hawkshaw.

MEG. The taxi driver!?

GEORGE. Yes. Yes, the taxi driver. Never been totally happy with him. Good to be back. Good to be back. You out now. Out.

RIDGWAY *walks to the exit.*

RIDGWAY. As we say in Manchester –

GEORGE *closes the door on him.*

GEORGE. And this time stay out. Don't all look so happy.
Hawkshaw's taxi receipts – go through them again. And the
witness statements, I want to know who saw what car. Was
he seen near any of the recent murders? Interviews from the
tape inquiry? Now. All the original statements. Look though
them properly. Parish records, registers for all the births.
Tidy up these fucking fivers –

MEG *discovers a mud-soaked coat within the Incident
Room.* GEORGE *snatches it out of her hands.*

GEORGE. No. No. No. No more attacks. We can't handle any
more until we've cleared this lot.

DICK. George, what do you want to do?

GEORGE. Deny it's one of his. Deny, deny, deny. Release
a statement advising – strongly advising that women – all
women – aren't to go out alone after nightfall. We'll put cars
out enforcing, nightly.

MEG. We can't do that.

GEORGE. Excuse me.

MEG. A curfew on women. It's the men we should be
focusing on.

GEORGE. Bring me a man who I can charge then. Who I can
arrest, who I can lock up and stop this all happening? Do
I want to tell me wife, my daughters, my colleagues, my
friends, my own team to stay inside? To hide? Because
I can't get to him? We're not talking hypotheticals. He will
kill again. How else can we make sure they'll be safe?

ANDY. We could ask Scotland Yard for help.

GEORGE. We're piling on, are we? Fuck the fucking Yard!
We've got a tape with his voice on it, letters –

MEG. Is no one going to say it?

DICK. We don't know about that tape. The information in the
letters, it was all in papers –

MEG. What if the letters are a hoax? The tape is a hoax? It's all fake?

GEORGE. What about the lab results? Where are they? Preston 75? The bite mark. We should interview everywhere that sells cassette tapes. Everywhere that –

MEG. Stop. Just stop.

GEORGE. You're the one who needs to stop, right now, sergeant. Christ. This room needs to be burnt down and started again, with a proper team. In the forces, you'd all be done for disobeying orders, for desertion. I'd have you all lined up against that wall and shot.

The whole room shakes.

SYLVIA. Did you feel that? It's like I'm drunk.

DICK. I felt it.

ANDY. Listen. There's a creaking sound.

MEG. It's the floor.

DICK. It's the bloody floor.

GEORGE. This is a new police station.

DICK. It's the weight of the paper. Get everything to the sides of the room. Now.

The whole team, except MEG *and* GEORGE, *try to move the tables to the side of the room.*

ANDY. It's too heavy. None of it will move.

DICK. Push harder! Come on.

The room is cleared to reveal a dress, left on scrub ground.

TELEVISION. November 18th, 1980. Jacqueline Hill, a twenty-year-old student at Leeds University was found murdered on scrub ground. Her handbag, found by a passerby stained with blood, was passed to the police. They conducted what is being described as 'a short search' which failed to find Jacqueline laid less than thirty yards away. Miss Hill is believed to have been struck from behind and dragged to the scrub ground where she was later discovered. Police are appealing to women in particular to look at their husbands, their sons, brothers, fathers and ask themselves if they could be the man responsible.

GEORGE *walks through the Incident Room, holding a box of his personal items.*

GEORGE. They're arriving tomorrow. Press officer's gone with 'super squad'. Handpicked men from Scotland Yard, from other forces, ordered by the Prime Minister herself. I'm sorry. I'll be back in uniform. Surprised it took them this long. I'm going to be in charge – in charge – of dogs, and horses. The police never forgive. Remember that. My career, it's over. There's one man to blame for that, and you're looking at him. I just wish we'd caught him. I sincerely wish you the very best of luck.

GEORGE *exits.*

Twenty-Four

A phone rings.

MEG. Millgarth Incident Room – What? Are you sure? Is it definitely the Ripper? Where?

She slams her hand on the table to get everyone's attention. We jump forward in time.

DICK. Sheffield!?

MEG. They picked him up last night in Sheffield, just a couple of uniformed beat officers. They found this car near the red-light district, man with a girl inside, they ran his plates through the system and while that was happening, this man, he went for a piss. It comes back the plates were false, So they arrested him.

DICK. Last night?

MEG. Yeah, they took him to their nick. He was uncomfortable, kept changing his story. So, they looked through his car and found a toolbox with all the gear you'd expect but no hammer. So they went back to where they'd arrested him, and where he'd gone for a piss they found one.

SYLVIA. Bloody hell.

MEG. And a knife. And when they asked him about it he said 'I think you've been building up to it,' and they say 'up to what?' And he said 'the Yorkshire Ripper' and they say 'what about him?' and he said 'well it's me.' And he's telling them everything. Everything. His name's Peter Sutcliffe.

ANDY. Peter William Sutcliffe?

MEG. Yeah.

ANDY. No. No!

SYLVIA. Andy? Andy!

ANDY. My report! The report I handed to you two years ago. I met him.

SYLVIA. What does he look like?

MEG. He's got size seven shoes, dark hair, beard and a gap in his teeth.

ANDY. And he doesn't have a Geordie accent. Here – look. You typed it for me.

MEG. I know.

DICK. God.

SYLVIA. But Andy, there have been hundreds of reports.

DICK. I'm heading there now, you better see how often his name crops up in this mess.

ANDY. I met him, I spoke to him, I sat in the man's house, and I knew.

MEG. Calm down.

ANDY. I'm going to get killed for this.

MEG. Nobody outside his room knows. And nobody outside this room is going to know.

ANDY. I should have pushed harder.

DICK (*slipping out of time*). When you run this over again, and again and again. Does he ever forgive me?

MEG. He idolised you.

DICK. I know.

MEG. He forgives you. A bit late. But he comes around, in the end. He even speaks at your –

DICK. At my funeral?

MEG. Yeah.

DICK. We all die eventually. Nothing to be sad about. I have to ask. The tape. The letters. The Geordie accent.

MEG. You don't want to know. They caught him in the end. On a DNA cold case in the 2000s. His name is John Humble. Not related to the case, in any way. Just a drunk.

DICK. Why did he do it?

MEG. When he was asked why he did it, he said it was because he was bored.

Long pause.

This'll tickle you. You're looking at, eventually, the first female Inspector of the West Yorkshire Police.

We're back in the Incident Room again.

DICK. You coming, Sylvia?

SYLVIA. I'm coming! I'm coming!

DICK. How long have we got?

MEG. She's got ten years.

DICK. Ten years. That's enough.

SYLVIA. When we get home tonight let's go to bed, and never get up again.

SYLIVA exits.

DICK. Sounds like heaven.

MEG. Mr Holland.

DICK. Inspector Winterburn.

DICK *exits*.

Twenty-Five

TISH *enters. It's just* MEG *and* ANDY *left now, clearing the room.*

MEG. Let me guess.

TISH. Guess what?

MEG. What you're going to ask me. Would I like to comment on what is fast being perceived as a complete bungle by the police? How we interviewed him numerous times –

TISH. Nine times. According to my sources.

MEG. If I, as a woman, and as a police officer feel that –

TISH. No, none of that. Just one question really: who is Andrew Laptew?

MEG. Where have you got that name from? Why do you want to know about Andy Laptew?

TISH. I've got a tip-off. That an Andy Laptew met Sutcliffe. Had suspicions. Years ago. Was ignored. And that three women went on to get killed.

There's a pause. It's clear MEG *isn't going to answer.* TISH *turns to* ANDY.

Do you know him?

ANDY. Yes. Who told you that? Who have you been speaking to?

TISH. Are you Andrew Laptew?

MEG. We need to take a step back here.

TISH. Stay out of this. Are you?

ANDY. I am.

MEG. This isn't fair. He can't talk to the press.

TISH. He doesn't have to say a word. I'm telling you, I know this information.

MEG. They'll think he's leaked it.

TISH. Andrew, Andy, listen to me. You know what I know. And I'm giving you warning now that I am going to publish it. If there's something I've said that's wrong, if there's a reason I shouldn't, take a sip of that cup of coffee. And I'll know. You don't need to say a word.

MEG. Andy –

TISH. Do you want some coffee, Andrew? Even just a sip?

ANDY *doesn't move*.

Right.

MEG. You'll ruin his career.

TISH. Of all the people to feel sorry for, you in the police are pretty much bottom of the list. Well, Andrew, Megan, I'll be seeing you.

MEG. In the *Daily Mirror*?

TISH. The *Sunday Times* these days. At least one of us – got what we wanted.

TISH *exits*.

MEG. Go after her. They'll think you leaked it.

ANDY. Career? I've not slept since he was caught. I don't deserve to.

ANDY *exits*. MEG *continues to clear the final boxes and papers*.

Epilogue

MAUREEN *enters, and watches* MEG, *her table covered in photographs of the victims, the final things to be filed away.*

MAUREEN. You were supposed to ring me. I don't know how to feel. Happy? I suppose. I thought where's the one place they won't be playing the news and showing his face over and over and over. And I was right, I bet you can't stand to look at him either. Bet you're binning everything.

MEG. It's being 'archived'.

MAUREEN. I'm still here though. In that terrible photograph. Not one of these is a good one. When you hear my name, do you think of me or this horrible mugshot?

MEG. I think of you. On one of our nights out undercover.

MAUREEN. You're the only one.

MEG. Since you told me about the graves, I make an effort to picture them all another way. Doing something every day, something normal, boring even.

MAUREEN. Like what?

MAUREEN *and* MEG *begin to archive the photographs.*

MEG. Wilma McCann, making herself some tea in the morning and spilling it into the saucer. Emily Jackson, listening to the radio, not wanting to get out of bed. Patricia Atkinson, running late, brushing her hair. Jayne MacDonald –

MAUREEN. With her friends, buying a new dress.

MEG. Jean Jordan, waiting for a bus, smiling to herself.

MAUREEN. Helen Rytka – painting her bedsit with her twin sister. Covered in bits of paint.

MEG. Josephine Whitaker opening some post, to find a cheque inside.

MAUREEN. Barbara Leach smoking a cigarette, having given up for a month.

MEG. Marguerite Walls laughing in the pictures, being shushed.

MAUREEN. I was going to say the pictures next.

MEG. Jacqueline Hill, walking across a park, just a woman, walking by herself, thinking thoughts all of her own.

MAUREEN. That just leaves me.

MEG. Maureen. That's easy. Maureen Long, life of the party, dressed up, hair perfect, face on, dancing and dancing and dancing, surrounded by people. And nobody –

Like ghosts, the room fills again with the STAFF OF THE INCIDENT ROOM.

MAUREEN. Yes?

MEG. – nobody knows who she is.

End.

www.nickhernbooks.co.uk

facebook.com/nickhernbooks

twitter.com/nickhernbooks